20 IDEAS

FOR TEACHING GIFTED KIDS IN THE MIDDLE SCHOOL & HIGH SCHOOL

**EDITED BY
JOEL MCINTOSH**

ISBN 1-882664-05-1

Prufrock
Press
Post Office Box 8813
Waco, Texas 76714-8813
1-800-998-2208

Table Of Contents

Introduction

If memory serves me, the idea for *The Journal of Secondary Gifted Education*, was born during a Sunday afternoon car trip. Just off I-35 between Dallas and Austin, lies Salado, Texas, a little town that boasts lots of antique shops and one of the best restaurants in the state—The Stagecoach Inn (if you go, ask for plenty of hush-puppies). It was to this restaurant that my wife and I were driving (we often took this hour-long trip for Sunday lunch).

As we traveled, we discussed a number of topics. One was a need that I was experiencing as a teacher of secondary gifted children. "There is just so little information and ideas available for secondary teachers of these students," I told my wife. "Of course, when I go to conferences and workshops, there are plenty of teachers doing some wonderful things with their kids, but you can only go to so many conferences. I just wish there were a journal just for teachers of secondary gifted students."

My wife, a magazine editor, smiled and said, "Why don't you and I publish one?" Giving birth to this idea was that simple.

Within a month, we had purchased our first desktop publishing system (a bargain-basement priced, Atari computer). By May of that year, we had lined-up articles for the first issue. In September, our first issue rolled off the press.

The finger crossing worked. Today, *JSGE* acts as the only international journal devoted to secondary teachers of gifted students. Each issue of the journal is read by over six-thousand teachers in the United States, Canada, and Australia. While our subscriber base has grown, the sophistication of our computer systems increased, and our staff made larger, we have never forgotten our original vision—to provide secondary teachers of gifted children with ideas and information they can apply to their classrooms.

This anthology is a chronicle of our first two years. We have included twenty of the more then sixty articles appearing in the journal during that time. Regrettably, some of the earlier articles are not included because they were "lost" in our transition from the Atari desktop publishing system to our present Macintosh system. My hope is that these lost articles might be included in a future edition of this book. Yet, this loss only affects the size of this book, not its present content. The articles included are superb. They are the work of educators across the nation who took their time to share their theories, research, and classroom successes. Their work is at the heart of *JSGE's* success.

— *J.E.M.*

Chapter 1

General Information
And Inspiration

Career Reflections
One Teacher Looks Back On A Career Changed By The Use Of Creative Teaching Strategies

By Paul DeKock

A Late August Reverie

Teaching juices beginning to bubble ... Empty classroom smells and images ... Retired at 58 two years ago after 31 years in the classroom ... Fulfilled but a gentle sadness remains because I'll never do again what I so much loved doing ...

Each August for the rest of my life, sepia memories of me in my classroom will play on my mind's movie screen, but I am now married to my Macintosh computer and my second career. I won't be going back.

I'm one of many newly retired teachers in their seventh decade who cherish memories of meeting teaching's daily challenges. I was fortunate. So many of the students whom I touched and who touched me were capable and caring. And while teaching my last 26 years in the same high school, I reached all the brothers and sisters in certain families and even taught sons and daughters of former students who fell in love in the same classroom a generation before.

Teaching was a continuing marvel for me because I blended my vocation and avocations. My multiple loves—our nation, our nation's literature, acting, music, design, still photography, video, psychology (particularly the human life cycle)—all fused during a long career in which I taught American Studies, a two-hour course combining American history, American literature, composition, and public speaking.

In 1963, when I was 33, I met David Yount, who became my American Studies team teaching partner for the next 25 years. We retired together in 1988 to devote full time to Interact, Inc., our educational publishing company, which grew out of our American Studies teaching careers.

At first we were traditional teachers. We mainly lectured and held full class discussions and individual tutorials. We loved the sounds of our voices and confrontations with keen, young minds. We always remained in control. We knew what young people needed to know. After all, we were liberal arts majors with solid academic backgrounds in several disciplines at fine colleges and universities such as Wabash, Minnesota, New Mexico, and Harvard.

But as the 1960s and its Black Revolution boiled across America, we grew less certain about always knowing all the answers. We sensed we had to get students more involved. We began questioning ourselves. What were our students really thinking? What kind of an America did they dream about shaping? Could we teach democracy if our students didn't practice democracy in our classrooms?

We agreed we had to find a way to reach more of our students. Gradually the number of lectures diminished. We met our students in seminar clusters. But we still sensed they needed to talk more to one another without our presence always leading or dominating. For a while we used the Harvard Business School case study model for instruction. Then suddenly, after Dave attended a workshop on simulations, we found the ideal vehicle. We would give students roles (historical or imaginary) within simulated environments. Our students experiencing Black history and literature would wear "two hats": real students and imaginary Black and White identities living in six varying neighborhoods in an modern city wracked by racial crises. As a result, after playing our Sunshine City simulation during the Watts Crisis, we had actual students graduate from high school and participate in voter registration drives in the South. For our students the school world interrelated with the real world.

In the years that followed, Dave and I used simulations and grouping strategies in our classes. Here are a few of the experiences our American Studies students had:

- a contemporary society paralleling the moral values of 17th century Puritans (Puritan history and literature);
- a 21st century cluster of states gradually moving from confederation to federation (the 1780s);
- re-creations of actual or imaginary historical events (Jefferson's Louisiana Decision; trials of John Brown, John Scopes, William Calley, Harry Truman; debates on annexing Mexico, acquiring the Philippines, or establishing an immigration Quota System);
- being 1900 immigrants and processors at Ellis Island (immigration history and literature);
- 1900 roles in a small town (Spoon River Anthology and Our Town);
- being farmers, labor leaders, businessmen, social critics, and legislators in the 1920s and 1930s (the stock market crash, the "First 100 Days" of the New Deal, The Great Gatsby and The Grapes of Wrath);
- deciding how simple they wished their lives to be at age 35 (Thoreau and the voluntary simplicity movement);

- historical and literary TV news casts (the Westward movement; ante-bellum literature);
- daily writing logs (notes they took—what they learned—and notes they made—what they felt about the notes they took ... and then assimilating such notes into short compositions and longer research essays)

I used the word fulfilled in my reverie above. I know Dave and I have a particular immortality (what Erik H. Erikson calls generativity) because the way we taught American Studies impacted our students' lives in a positive way. We gave up on coverage. We decided to teach more by teaching less. We taught less literature and less history, but our students experienced more because they continually actively related the history and literature to their lives. Our curriculum had an existential center. We didn't pound information into their heads that they would promptly forget. Instead our students experienced cooperative learning and an integrated curriculum in which they took extensive writing notes that included their reflections upon the ideas and events' significance to their lives. Thus, they didn't rent our course; they owned it.

But, perhaps most important of all, they grew as human beings! Because they had to write and speak every day, they learned to communicate convictions and doubts to their classmates. If a person ever said "Anyone?" as in the film *Ferris Bueller's Day Off*, the person was a student; the person was not Dave or me. Thus, our classes became democratic communities where students were real to one another. Everyone learned as much process as content. Students didn't feel like sponges absorbing teacher wisdom. Instead they felt respected as young persons moving toward more sharply focused adult identities.

Today while representing our company, Dave and I enter many classrooms. Usually when we leave elementary classrooms, we remark about the energy of the participatory environment we just saw. There the teachers have committed themselves to organizing learning. On the other hand, too often when we leave secondary classrooms, we comment on how the environment reveals a teacher commitment to teaching information. And we ask, "How long will any of those young persons remember a lecture on the date and contents of the Treaty of Paris or the five elements of transcendentalism? One week? Two months? Wouldn't the educational effect be longer lasting if the students were actively using the information in some meaningful way?"

I wish I could wave a wand and place many of you secondary teachers out there in my former shoes. A movie begins replaying on my mind's movie screen ...

Students role-playing city council members from their neighbor-hoods are leaning forward in their desks. They are listening to 'Black' and 'White' classmates standing by an overhead projector and pointing to proposed school district boundaries for their imaginary community. Their arguments are rooted in controversies over *Plessy v. Ferguson* and *Brown v. Topeka*. A student passionately speaks about "those black and white dolls and the psychological damage resulting from that 'separate but equal' stupidity." Students aren't prattling. They are using arguments that Earl Warren's court members heard in 1954 ...

I smile. I remember my inner glow at that moment in the 1960s. I miss the glow, but I have the memory.

After you retire, what do you want to remember?

Paul DeKock and David Yount spent the final decades of their teaching careers at El Capitan High School in Lakeside, California. If you are interested in obtaining information about the K-12 simulations and other cooperative learning materials that their company publishes, write for catalogs c/o Interact, Box 997, Lakeside, California 92040.

Map Design And Redesign
Sometimes A Loss Puts
What We Do In Perspective

By Kathryne Lewis

All teachers have a group of "special students" that are unlike any they have ever taught. For one reason or another, they sneak up on you, and then they steal your heart.

My group came at a time in my career when I was considering giving up teaching. I felt I was just too tired to make a difference anymore. Then, this group of twenty young people entered my life. They were loud and quiet, rowdy and gentle, brilliant and impossible. And, they were the most sensitive, caring, tenacious, and infuriating group of students I have encountered in twenty years of classroom teaching.

One of them, Dawn, died last year, and it is in her memory that I write this article. In coping with her death, I asked myself, "What would Dawn have me say about teaching gifted students? What would she have me say about life?" The answer is painful, but I'll try to share it.

First, life is fragile—handle it with love. But, how do we love kids and still be the kind of teacher we know we should be? By doing just that—by being the kind of teacher we know we should be. We must be tough—have stringent rules, have uncompromising convictions, and standards that are high enough to encourage real thought and mental growth. We must be gentle, knowing that no rule applies 100 percent, all the time. We must recognize that our convictions are not their convictions, and that our standards are not their standards.

The beauty lies in helping students to discover strong convictions of their own and to develop standards that will last through the good and bad times in their lives. We must be prepared to "teach our hearts out" even when students don't seem to care, and we must "care" even when we don't want to.

Educational excellence is a given. There can be no compromises in the quality of work we expect from our students. Likewise, we must help them realize the inner strength it takes to be uncompromising in their personal lives as well.

Gifted students often feel responsible for so many things, and indeed they are, but only to a point. We must help our students realize that theirs is a great challenge—to be all that they can be in serving their fellow human and in bettering their world. Yet, they must remain true to themselves and their own goals and beliefs. Learning this kind of lesson often takes a lifetime, but with the pressures put on gifted students today, this lesson is of primary importance for their very survival. We must teach this lesson very early in their lives. I can still see Dawn's magnificent eyes looking at me, searching me to see just how much I would push her. And, to see just how much I was willing to compromise myself. Did I only talk a good game, or I was I true to my beliefs. No one in that classroom could escape Dawn's scrutiny—not judgment, appraisal. She rarely said anything, but her eyes helped keep us all on track.

Second, life is fragile—handle it with love. Dawn truly believed in the dignity of the individual. And, what an individual she was! Like so many gifted people, she simply would not bend to the will of others. She drove me insane with her obstinacy. She was an artist, and would not be bullied into being anything else, and she would not hear of taking the SAT (a mistake she later admitted). I could not talk her into applying to colleges just because lucrative scholarships were available. She methodically chose the school most appropriate for her and went about securing the funds to go there. The fact that she did not enroll there disappointed us both, but then Dawn had a way all of her own. She encouraged those students around her who pursued scholarships and went straight to college, but she never lost her own self-worth as she struggled to find her own path.

We struggled with her, knowing that she would eventually discover her way, and she almost made it. Almost.

Today, I ask myself if there had been a way to help her find more viable choices than she made. She had such a gift for words. Had I done a better job of career counseling, she might have made wiser choices. But, Dawn would want no recrimination. She openly accepted herself and those around her for the essence of their humanness—for the "insides of their souls" she used to say. She helped me remember the idealism of earlier years, the belief that every individual is important to this Earth, that each person's gifts are unique and should be valued.

But hers was a long and arduous search. She was hurt and lonely many times. Reality was hard on her, and yet it was her friend. Someone once said, "The worst lie is to lie to yourself." Dawn never lost sight of the realities in her life; yet, she never gave up on her dreams. And, though her path was far from straight, she never discontinued her journey; she just redesigned her map and went on.

Finally, life is fragile—handle it with love. Dawn never gave up on humanity. She was one of those unique people who has an unwavering faith in tomorrow. She believed what scripture tells us, "Love is patient, love is kind, and is not jealous; love does not brag and is not arrogant, does not act unbecoming; it does not seek its own, is not provoked, does not take into account a wrong suffered, does not rejoice in unrighteousness, but rejoices with the truth; bears all things, hopes all things, endures all things."

Love hopes and endures—that doesn't mean we should be gullible or "taken in" by the myriad of smoke screens that our students put up for us. What it does mean is that we must never quit believing that change can occur, that students can reach their potential, that we can make a difference. All things are possible to some degree or another. It is our vision that must remain intact. We must be as tenacious in our beliefs as we want our students to be, and then we must model that tenacity.

As teachers we can never lose hope. And, we must somehow instill the belief in our students that they must never lose hope. I have sat in the teachers lounge on occasion and heard teachers talk about how they can hardly wait to "burst that kid's bubble" or "put him in his place." Such talk makes me furious. Bubbles will burst soon enough and places are to be discovered, not imposed. Our job is to teach students to be "possibility" thinkers, not bound by the restraints of pessimism. Love hopes—it believes all things. Dawn believed in life. I agree with her.

So what does this say to me as a teacher—as a person. We are teaching human beings with complex emotional needs and values. My class of twenty students would not allow me to categorize them or put them in easy boxes or pigeonholes. Thank goodness. My job with them was, and still is, to bring some structure to their learning environment, guide them to challenges, and turn them loose to learn in my classroom and throughout their lives. In doing so, I began to know them and care about them and the "insides of their souls" more than anything in that classroom.

I taught that group of twenty, nurtured them, and pushed them as hard as possible, never forgetting who they were as individuals, and as a wonderful group of gifted kids. We challenged each other to remember that dreams really do come true—if we make them come true, if we refuse to let them go.

As I think back on the years I spent with those students, I am not sure which of us learned the most. I certainly didn't leave education; I didn't give up on my dream. Yet, like Dawn, I have redesigned the map.

Just thinking about those students relights a fire. Just thinking about Dawn touches my soul.

Author's note: Dawn Woodmansee was taken suddenly ill in June, 1990. Less than one week later she died from what should have been a routine illness.

A classroom teacher for twenty years and a teacher of gifted students for six, Kathryne Lewis is currently an Instructional Officer for Tomball School District, Tomball, TX 77375.

Start Early And Avoid The Mid-Winter Blues
A Few, Easy Steps Any G/T Teacher
Can Take To Avoid Burn-Out

By Kathryne Lewis

For the last seven years, I have attended seminars, conferences, college classes, and sermons regarding the care and feeding of gifted students. I have been encouraged, discouraged; lifted up, torn down; inspired, demoralized. And, I have asked myself more than once lately ... but what about the G/T teachers? What about our care and feeding?

With the increased spotlight on gifted education, teachers are being given the complex tasks of writing curricula, selecting materials, screening G/T program entrants, doing lunch duty, meeting with parents, organizing PTA meetings, and then—somehow—teaching gifted students.

Most G/T teachers typically set very high standards for themselves. They feel they must be a combination of Mother Theresa, Captain Kangaroo, and Atilla the Hun. But, the stress to succeed can lead quickly to burn-out. Too often, just about the time G/T teachers figure out how to do the kind of job they would like to do, they are just too tired to do it. To help you avoid this fate, I would like to suggest a few practical steps which have helped me survive the toughest times.

First, because we often establish our own domain once that classroom door shuts and instruction begins, teaching G/T students can be a very lonely experience. G/T teachers need each other (and, at times, much prayer). To overcome this isolation, form a network of G/T teachers—a support group that can give strength, advice, consolation, and encouragement.

No one knows what teaching is all about until he has taught. Likewise, no teacher knows what teaching the gifted is like until they have taught the gifted. They have little idea what it is like to cope with the joys and challenges of students selected for a program based upon their exceptional mental ability, creativity, and leadership skills. Some days just getting these students to sit down is a challenge.

When I began teaching a class for gifted students six years ago, I was the only G/T teacher on my campus. Talk about lonely! Fortunately for me, there were two other teachers in my district who were involved in gifted education. We took classes together, spent hours planning programs, and met weekly throughout the school year (sometimes meeting for a few minutes was all that we needed). We learned so much together, and we developed a unity that still flows throughout our district's G/T program five years later.

One particularly helpful activity developed in my school district was a county-wide meeting of G/T teachers and administrators. We divided sessions by grade level and curriculum area and organized a special session for administrators. We invited speakers, and appointed team leaders to lead workshops and sharing sessions (everyone brought something to share). This type of meeting proved to be so successful that it has continued for several years. Cost and preparation time are minimal and the results are fantastic.

Another particularly helpful tactic includes semi-annual planning sessions conducted in January and June. Led by the G/T coordinator, these meetings allow teachers to share concerns about the program and to identify goals for future instructional planning. We clarify instructional goals for K-12 and get a chance to share two positive things that have happened in our classrooms during the previous school year. We hold these meetings strictly to an hour and a half, and when that time is up, the meeting is over. Although these meetings are not required, no one wants to miss them.

While a network of other teachers will offer great support, it is not enough. You must keep in mind that great teachers are always the individuals able to take whom they are and develop a teaching style that is personally successful. You are an important individual with your own interests. With this in mind, it helps if you can plan to sandwich some of your favorite units of study between those intense, pressure driven units you feel you simply "must" teach. When I experience this type of pressure cooker instruction for an extended period of time, I take a day with my students and study a favorite poem or quotation. By doing this, I find that not only do I come away refreshed, but my students do too.

Also, as G/T teachers, we must learn the art of the possible. Too often, some G/T teachers see themselves as the be all and end all of their students' educational experiences. Consequently, these teachers are filled with guilt discreetly concealed behind their grade books and their copies of a teacher appraisal instrument. Let's face it—we are real teachers living in a real world. We simply cannot do it all—nor should we. When we make ourselves the center of responsibility for our students' educational universe, we rob them of the opportunity to become self-directed and independent learners.

Worse still, we establish a situation where no one really wins. Other teachers become isolated from us because we are so busy trying to stay one step ahead of the students. Our students begin wanting to have learning done to them instead of becoming autonomous learners, and our administrators just avoid us as much a possible. To circumvent this, we must know our strengths, our weaknesses, what we want to accomplish, what we have to accomplish, and what we might accomplish if we work really hard.

One year I set what I considered a moderate goal for my English I G/T class—something like reading every short story known to man (or so my students complained). By the end of the second week of a four week unit, we all hated short stories. We were doing so much reading and intense discussion of literary import that we were not enjoying the beauty and excitement of the works. So we came to a screeching halt, re-evaluated our goals, and decided to cut the remainder of our reading list considerably—keeping works we simply had to read and the ones we wanted to enjoy. The trade off was one of quantity for quality. We slowed down the pace, took a week longer to finish the unit, and had a wonderful learning experience (learning not only about short stories but about goal setting as well).

Sometimes the concept of the art of the possible is hard to grasp. We want to do so much. We want prepared students. But, when we can tie our lofty dreams to solid reality, we can achieve so much more, and live to tell about it.

The survival answers for G/T teachers are astoundingly clear and as ancient as teaching itself. We must value our inner light as much as we value the inner light of our students. We must join together to support the idealism inherent in gifted education, and, of greatest importance, we must strive to make our dreams become reality.

A classroom teacher for twenty years and a teacher of gifted students for six, Kathryne Lewis is currently an Instructional Officer for Tomball School District, Tomball, TX 77375.

Chapter 2

Math & Science

Independent Research
In Math And Science
A Program For Gifted Young
Scientists And Mathematicians

By Melanie Krieger

To better meet the needs of its gifted students, Ward Melville High School in Melville, N.Y., has instituted a new course known as West Prep. West Prep is a course in independent, scientific research in math and science for high ability learners.

In the course, students work on major research projects in all areas of math, science, and the social sciences. They study statistics and research methods, and they learn to write mathematical and scientific papers and to present those papers. These students enter their research in many scientific competitions such as the Westinghouse International Science and Engineering Fair and the New York State Energy Competition.

The core of the course revolves around major research projects conducted by students. Students are involved with the course for three years. They work on projects either in the high school or with mentors at Stony Brook University (a university that is within easy commuting distance from Ward Melville High School).

Science research projects are quite different from the projects that are usually found at a junior or senior high school science fair. These investigations are not simple models (a volcano, the ear, the solar system, etc.), collections of objects (rock and fossil collections), or reports (the heart, how oxygen aids combustion). The projects are independent research experiments conceived, designed, and conducted by the students using the scientific method.

For example, my students have worked on such projects as "Testing the Effects of Suggestion on Perception" and "Control of Growth Patterns: The Response of Bean Roots to Centrifugal Force and Gravity." Though such projects are interesting and exciting, there is much hard science behind them. West Prep students receive a thorough grounding in the use of the scientific method, research designs, and statistical procedures. The scientific method is emphasized throughout the program.

While conducting research projects, students:

• State a hypothesis to define the problems they wish to solve.

- Design an experiment that allows the students to accept or reject the hypothesis.
- Construct an experimental set-up.
- Conduct the experiment and collect data.
- Analyze the data using statistical methods.
- Write and publish a paper about the experiment.

While the procedures students use when developing their research project are an essential part of the West Prep curriculum, getting started on a science research project that will be entered into a science competition can seem the most daunting to students new to the program. In truth, it is rare to just wake up one morning and say, "I know what problem I want to do research on." Most students have no idea how to find a project topic, much less a very specific science research problem.

The following is a list of suggestions I offer my own students upon first entering West Prep:

- Read as much as possible—magazines and books on the topic of science abound. In fact, a new magazine, *Quantum*, designed specifically for gifted science and math students is now available.
- Find out about the scientific lectures, symposia, science fairs, and conferences in your area. GO!
- Visit as many local industries, utility companies, and museums as possible. The computer department, quality control, and design and engineering departments are interesting areas to visit.
- Discover the student science programs in your area. There may be Saturday morning workshops, laboratory experiences, lectures, or even courses for high school students.
- Find out about the science departments at your closest university. Visit! Call and speak to professors in the areas that seem interesting to you. Many professors will be glad to discuss their own experiments with you.
- Find out about the kinds of science courses offered at your local university. It might be possible for you to take a course there. Some universities and high schools have even developed programs in which high school students take college courses and receive concurrent credit for their work.
- Find a mentor. Survey the people around that can help you with your project. In many high schools, teachers have advanced degrees in specialized areas or have particular interests. Also, mentors can be found at universities and in industry.

- Create a science club. You may discover that some of your friends also want to enter a science research competition. If that is the case, they you may wish to form a science club. A club may become involved with all the previous activities and many others.

Students in West Prep discover that an independent science research project can be a very demanding undertaking. A research experiment involves much work, time, and effort. Yet, their time is well spent. Students can expect many benefits from research projects.

One of the most evident benefits of a research project is the knowledge acquired by students about specific topics that extend far beyond traditional curriculum. Whatever students choose to study: mathematical chaos and fractions, the motion of ocean waves, brine shrimp, nerve muscles, cell regeneration, or even political change, the acquired knowledge gained will far outdistance the standard curriculum.

As students work on their science research projects, they discover that the most important aspects of research are the new discoveries made and the exchange of ideas. To share these discoveries and ideas, they learn how to write a research paper and abstract. If the research proves to be successful, scientific journals may even publish their papers. Several of my students have had their research published in scientific journals in their fields of research. Students also learn how to present their own work either by giving talks before a large audience in a lecture hall or by making poster presentations.

Students find that they are able to meet to explain their work with distinguished scientists and judges. Students discuss their work with scientific experts and other judges at local and state science fairs, the annual International Science and Engineering Fair, and the finals of the Westinghouse Science Talent Search Competition. My students have discussed their research with field scholars, college professors, politicians, and even Nobel Prize winning scientists.

Science research projects and competitions can be financially rewarding. Many colleges offer merit scholarships to high school graduates who have worked on science research projects and entered the major science competitions. Also, many students receive internships in various university laboratories. They use the skills and techniques they have acquired while working on their research projects to continue their scientific explorations during their undergraduate years. Many of my students have received either direct financial aid for their science research or are carrying out the work study portions of their financial aid packages in the university laboratory.

Of course, many science research competitions award generous scholarships to competition winners. My students have received scholarships from the Westinghouse Science Talent Search Competition, the International Science and Engineering Fair, and professional organizations such as Sigma Xi, a scientific research society.

As the students work on their science research projects, they discover that they are acquiring benefits that they did not initially expect. Students are pleasantly surprised to discover that professional scientists are happy and willing to talk to them about their topics and research. These scientists and researchers do not treat the students as high school "kids," but as people whose enthusiasm, intelligence, and work they respect. Student researchers receive responsibilities and privileges equal to college students working in the research laboratory.

Working on a science research project can help students see the kind of work that they might do as an adult. Research should be much the same, whether the student begins it in high school, college, or graduate school

Also, student researchers are able to create better college applications. As they begin considering college applications and scholarships, they discover that there are many other highly qualified students competing with them. They find that there are many other valedictorians, salutatorians, and students in the top 5% of their classes competing for similar goals. Yet, successful participation in a research project is a unique advantage for students. Many of my previous students are currently working at Princeton University, M.I.T., the University of Pennsylvania, and Johns Hopkins University.

Yet, most important, students develop the skills, motivations, and interests that will allow them to become lifelong learners. Winning a science competition becomes less important than doing it. Students discover that they have won long before they have even entered.

Science And Mathematics Competitions

The following is a list of major competitions throughout the United States.

The Dupont Challenge
Science Essay Awards Program
Science Essay Awards Program
c/o General Learning Corporation
60 Revere Drive, Suite 200
Northbrook, IL 60062-1563

Duracell Scholarship Competition
Duracell Scholarship Competition
National Science Teachers Association
1742 Connecticut Avenue, NW
Washington, DC 20009

International Science and Engineering Fair
Science Service
1719 N. Street NW
Washington, DC 20036

Junior Science and Humanities Symposium
Academy of Applied Science
98 Washington Street
Concord, NH 03301

Space Science Student Involvement Program
Space Science Student Involvement Program
National Science Teachers Association
1742 Connecticut Avenue, NW
Washington, DC 20009

Thomas Edison/Max McGraw Scholarship Program
National Supervisors Association
Leadership Institute for Science Education Center
c/o Copernicus Hall, Room 227
Central Connecticut State University
1615 Stanley Street
New Britain, CT 06050

Westinghouse Science Talent Search Competition
Science Service
1719 N. Street, NW
Washington, DC 20036

Melanie Krieger is an educational consultant at Ward Melville High School in Melville, NY 11747. She has just completed her book, How to Excel in Science Competitions *to be published by Franklin Watts Inc.*

Producing Ideas In Mathematics
Encouraging Problem Solving Techniques
In The Mathematics Classroom

By Dr. M. Ann Dirkes

By third grade most students have figured out what is expected of them in mathematics and decide what they expect of themselves. Some are reflective by nature. Others are content with quick recall and the direct application of rules and algorithms (Garofalo, 1989). A teacher working with highly capable students described the modus operandi:

- Expect immediate results. Aim to be "finished."
- Write only what is required. Use numbers and other symbols with very few words and no drawings.
- Use only memorized steps.
- Stop thinking at the end of the steps.

These students tend to resist prolonged thinking and depend on a narrow approach to learning and doing mathematics.

Problem solvers, however, see their roles differently and have different expectations for themselves. Their outlook stretches to a broader perception of learning.

- Look for ideas that are not stated.
- Use drawings frequently. Discuss possibilities.
- State questions meaningfully and find many ways to approach each situation.
- Complex mathematics and new situations are not finished in one sitting. There is always more to say and more to understand.

Because this approach is comprehensive and runs counter to the experience of many students, it requires explanation and much support. Taking time to understand is annoying for students who believe that uncertainty and open-endedness are to be avoided (Doyle, 1983). These students must undergo a certain transformation before they embrace ambiguity as an opportunity for learning and open-endedness as an invitation to create knowledge. This means that students must begin monitoring their own thinking strategies and representations (Sternberg, 1985) as well as the pace of instruction.

Elements of a program designed to foster thinking in mathematics (Dirkes, in press) are outlined in this article. The program integrates the communications and connections recommended for studying mathematics along with a strong emphasis on problem solving (NCTM, 1989).

Students must become problem solvers if they are to excel in the mathematics required for new technologies and the changing milieu of everyday life. To prepare for these experiences, mathematics instruction must involve students in more than rules and definitions. In addition to reproducing prior knowledge, problem solvers make connections and produce new insights.

When a student says, "I don't know the answer," a teacher or peer should say, "What *do* you know about the situation?" Sensing ambiguity, students should remind themselves, "I know something about this. What is it, and what else do I know?" A habit of producing ideas replaces passivity or "giving up." The goal is for students to value understanding and connection-making over automatic routine.

With experience, students learn to make deliberate and forced connections. As they become searchers who wonder about possibilities, their thinking stretches out to more and more factors. They begin to consider probing questions. Such questions go beyond a simple search for correct procedures or steps.

- Should the answer be smaller than a given quantity? For example, 2/3 of 3/5 is part of 3/5.
- Does a word problem deal with division by 3 as "groups of 3" or as "3 equal groups"? Would repeated subtraction on a calculator handle the situation better?
- How is x/3 + xy/6 like 1/3 + 1/6? Should I divide 3 into 6 as I usually begin or would multiplying x/3 by 2/2 serve the purpose better?

Probing questions and unusual observation stimulate small group discussions and suggest changes in performance assessment.

- Why does .1 + .9 = 1
- Use graph paper to illustrate 3 cm2. What did you think about first—a drawing or a formula?
- Draw and label something to show why perimeter and area have different kinds of units.
- Draw something to show how 2/3 ÷ 1/4 and 6 ÷ 2 have the same meaning for division.
- Begin with point P on graph paper. Mark all of the points that are 3 cm from P.

- Estimate: 199/199 x 6 + 34 x 234/234 - 234/235 + 43/2.

In each case students are asked to produce what they know and test its connection to a given situation. Some students produce connections fluently and without direction. Others, however, need to be reminded to stretch their thinking.

Three strategies integrate productive thinking and learning: idea listing on a concept, reading mathematics to understand, solving word problems using modified idea listing.

Idea listing sessions are one way to encourage students to produce connections freely and to communicate them. This is brainstorming that is directed toward mathematical outcomes. Students learn to defer judgment during these sessions so that they focus instead on the generation of ideas. The production of a large number of ideas usually yields better ideas than a brief list.

Idea listing identifies what students know before they hear a teacher's presentation on a topic and before they are ready to measure their abilities on a test. It fosters confidence and raises questions or insights meaningful to students. Teachers use the lists to diagnose misconceptions and to analyze advanced understanding.

To develop a sense of fluency and original thinking, the first session for a group centers on a familiar topic (e.g., cars). Next, students learn that they can become as fluent connecting mathematical concepts to other mathematics, other disciplines, and the world at large.

It is best to select a broad mathematical topic (e.g., fractions, measurement, tens, area, algebraic substitutions, or graphing a straight line). The strategy checklist shown in Table 1 directs thinking toward mathematical concerns.

Table 1

Sentences with =, <, >
Examples
Estimates
Drawings
Definitions
Patterns
Unusual Ideas
Uses
Spatial Observations
Other

Students refer to the checklist after they have exhausted the ideas that come to mind quickly at the beginning of an idea listing session. Inventive students revise the list according to their assumptions about the nature of mathematics. Discussions about what mathematics is and what thinking is contribute well to the development of appropriate attitudes and goals.

During large group sessions, the teacher lists ideas on the chalkboard. In small group sessions, one person suggests categories on the checklist and discourages discussion and judgment. Another student writes the ideas expressed by group members. Ideas spoken aloud usually stimulate new ideas in the listeners.

Students identify the "best" ideas after the list has multiple entries. Usually, the greater the challenge a situation presents, the longer the list of ideas that students need to generate before they find connections that represent new understanding. Those who list many ideas discover that they know much more than they anticipate.

A classroom test might consist of one question, "List as many ideas as you can about percentage. Refer to the Strategy Checklist and list ideas under these categories—Representations, Uses, and Other."

Students know that the test will be scored according to the number of non-repeated ideas generated from many points of view. To indicate the score, teachers underline entries liberally. Most instances of remote or uncertain relevance are counted, and incorrect entries are ignored. Extra points can be assigned for procedures emphasized during instruction (e.g., drawings, charts) and points can be subtracted for an important concept omitted. It is not necessary for students to indicate the checklist strategy and there is no penalty for listing ideas under a less appropriate category.

An idea list on percentage might include the entries in Figure 1. Although students produce many of the same ideas, lists from different students demonstrate the diversity of their experiences and the new connections they are able to make.

Like idea listing, reading and rereading texts increases the time students spend thinking. "What does the author say about the graph in the textbook?" "What do you think it means?" "What else could be said about it?" These are the type of questions asked in social studies and literatures courses. They contribute to the development of mathematics as well.

The concern is that students learn mathematics by reading about concepts and by studying procedures. A college-bound high school senior was enrolled in an advanced mathematics course that used a self-paced system requiring much reading and self-direction. At the end of the year, he observed, "This is the first time in my life that I have read a math book." In other mathematics courses, he could learn well enough to score high on tests by listening to teachers and doing the examples on homework assignments.

A student activity on the effect of the constant in $y = ax + b$ (Figure 2) illustrates how reading and producing ideas require that students think for themselves. The activity is written under an assumption that students have had no class presentation on the topic. Prior activities, however, introduced graphing lines. A question at the end of the activity calls for conjecture or generalizations. The less direct a question is, the more that students should expect to use their own ideas without restriction.

Other tips for doing activities like this one include labeling, rereading, idea listing, discussions with a peer, and frequent use of graph paper (also for problems that do not use coordinate axes). Students are encouraged to experiment with ideas. They do activities as if they were writing notes for themselves rather than for a teacher's evaluation.

A word problem is a challenge because it is complex, with many facts and variables; or it is novel, a new experience for the problem solver. Complexity and novelty call for self-direction. This includes idea listing from different points of view, reading, drawing, and time for incubation. Most important, challenge questions, as well as open-ended ones, call for conjectures. These are possibilities that might lead to significant insights. If students claim that they do not need to conjecture, then the question is not a problem or challenge for them.

Problem solving deals primarily with four major areas: facts; the question or objective; ideas produced to reach the objective; and a check on the agreement among facts, question, and answer. Students usually know that they should examine the facts given in a word problem. They can also add probable names and conditions that clarify the context of the problem. Restating the question in their own language clarifies the goal. Idea listing extends the search to new connections and possibilities. The evaluation step certifies that the objective has been reached.

Mathematics becomes more meaningful to some students when they use words instead of graphics, charts, and symbols. Giving them an option to express their ideas in paragraphs at the beginning of a difficult problem boosts their willingness to think. All students benefit from their own word descriptions of what problem solving means to them.

Another approach is to have students use the problem solving steps to create problems themselves. Given a few facts in a problem situation, students add other factors and ask a question. Monitoring the

Figure 1
An Idea List On The Topic Of Percentages

Representations

10%   3%

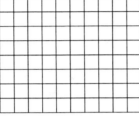   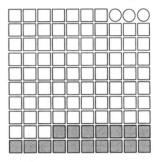

per hundred, division   3% = .03 = .1 x 30%
part of 100   % has 2 zeros like 100
100% = 1.0   3 out of 100 = 3%
200% is twice as much   3% + 17% = 20%, 2 rows

Uses
- Discount
- Interest to pay on bor-rowed money
- Interest to receive on investments
- Field goals made out of total tried
- Batting average .300 = 30%
- Part of last year's sales reported
- Scores greater than the mean on a test

Other
- Probability of 1:2 is a 50% chance
- 14/29 is about 50
- A dime is 10% of a dollar
- $1.00 = 100 pennies like 100 percent
- 1.6% = .016

Student's Total Score = 22

complexity of the question posed is part of the development of prob-lem solving. The work is evaluated in much the same way as idea list-ing. The more complex, original, and extensive the work, the higher the evaluation. The best environment, however, is one in which stu-dents value the art of problem solving over scoring reliability. The inherent difficulty of evaluating real problem solving should not pre-vail over the thinking process.

Figure 2
Reading Activity

1. To see a "higher" line:
   a. Graph: y = x
      Call it x = y.
   b. Raise every point one unit higher.

      (0,0)(1,1)(3,3)(4,4)   x = y
      (0,1)(1,2)(3,4)(5,6)   ? = y

   c. Write something about x and y in (0,1).
      Does your idea apply to (1,2) and (3,4)?
      Write: On the higher line, x + 1 = ? for all points.

2. a. Graph: y = 2x
      Begin with (0,0) and (2,4)
   b. To graph y = 2x + 1:
      Make all points on y = 2x higher.
      One point is (0,1).

3. a. Graph: y = 1/2x
      Begin with (0,0) and (4,2).
   b. Graph: y = 1/2x + 3

4. a. Graph: y = x and y = x + 3 on the same axes.
   b. Graph: y = 2x and y = 2x + 3
   c. Graph: y = 1/2x and y = 1/2x + 5

5. List a few ideas about graphs like y = x and y = x + 1.

Instruction that develops problem solving and inquiry is still under development. Educators are not as equipped to develop the kinds of thinking that problem solvers use as we are to reinforce simple recall and the automatic application of algorithms. Teachers are encouraged, therefore, to search for new ways to have students experience mathematics.

Three strategies have been described in this article—idea listing on concepts, reading mathematics with idea production, and solving word problems in a productive mode. These strategies develop thinking in ways unfamiliar to many students whether or not they score high on standardized achievement tests.

As students produce ideas original to themselves and think with persistence, teachers respect their efforts and respond with a supportive reward system. Students, in turn, begin looking forward to the challenges this approach offers.

Yet, the culture established in most schools does not make the job of implementing this approach a simple one. This task requires a program that changes habits and increases individual effort. With new expectations for students and opportunities for self-direction, however, the teacher-student teams in schools can develop a problem solving approach to learning. This means that students monitor their thinking and choose productive strategies that maximize their accomplishments. Teachers develop a new perception of mathematical thinking and initiate appropriate learning activities. For those ready for the challenge, this program can become a significant contribution to the education of students.

Works Cited

Dirkes, M.A. (In press). *Producing ideas in mathematics*. Buffalo: D.O.K. Publishers.

Doyle, W. (1983). "Academic work." *Review of educational research*, 53(2), 159-199.

Garofalo, J. (1989). "Beliefs, responses, and mathematics education: observations from the back of the classroom." *School science and mathematics*, 89(6), 451-455.

National Council of Teachers of Mathematics. (1989). *Curriculum and evaluation standards for school mathematics*. Reston: NCTM.

Parnes, S. (1981). *Magic of your mind*. Buffalo: Creative Education Foundation.

Sternberg, R. (1985). *Beyond I.Q*. Cambridge: Cambridge University.

M. Ann Dirkes, Ed.D. is currently a professor of education at Purdue University at Fort Wayne. Her book Producing Ideas in Mathematics *will be available from D.O.K. Publishers in late spring of 1991.*

Science And The Fine Arts
An Entertaining Method For Teaching The Sciences

By Renata Otterbach

At a recent gifted and talented convention, I attended a presentation which included a panel of gifted students discussing their G/T programs. One part of the discussion grabbed the attention of both the audience and myself:

"What is the most boring subject you take?"

"Science. All we ever do is repeat experiments that someone else has already done."

The comment amazed me. I always thought letting the students conduct a variety of challenging experiments was something they enjoyed, especially when these experiments were combined with interesting discussions of scientific issues. But, in this student's opinion, that was not sufficient. The phrase that kept coming back to me was "repeat experiments that someone else has already done." This student was looking for the opportunity to do something new, something different.

Prior to the convention I had been working on some materials combining science with drama. Maybe these materials could be modified to meet the needs of the gifted and talented students.

I had some examples of my new materials with me, so after the panel discussion was over, I showed them to the student and asked his opinion. While I waited, he read through them and went to his mother to share them with her. The materials fascinated the two.

The materials consisted of two parts—skits teaching basic information and questions with activities that reinforce and expand the concepts taught.

For instance, an introductory lesson on viruses might include the skit "Interview With A Virus" (see box).

Skits like this can be used in a variety of ways. One way is to make a time-line based on your lesson plans and assign skits for presentation on an appropriate day as a focus activity. Another possibility is to use the skit within the classroom in a reader's theater format. They could also be used as a silent reading activity for the first five or ten minutes of class and then discussed thereafter.

Regardless of the method used to read the skit, it lends itself to questions that range from the lowest levels of Bloom's taxonomy to the highest. Below are some of the sample questions that might accompany the skit above.

- What are viruses made of?
- What do viruses do when they are outside a cell?
- What do viruses do when they are inside a cell?
- How are viruses different from cells?
- How are viruses like cells?
- Why do you think a virus would dislike a scientist?
- What else would you like to know about viruses, and how would you find out?
- Pretend that you are a scientist. Would you have acted the same as the scientist in the script? Give your reasons for why or why not.
- If you could talk to a virus, what are some questions you would ask?
- Pretend you are a virus and you keep a diary of your daily life. What are some of the things you would write?

Scientist:	You know for a non-living thing you sure create enough problems!
Virus:	Who says that I am non-living?
Scientist:	I do. All you are is a protein coat of DNA. You can't do anything unless you are in a cell. Now, a cell, that is a living thing. It has its own unique structure, and ...
Virus:	(*Interrupt*) I have my own unique structure.
Scientist:	(*Ignores interruption*) It moves, takes in food, carries on respiration and reproduction.
Virus:	I reproduce.
Scientist:	That's all you can do, and then you take over and mess everything up.
Virus:	I don't think things get messed up. Everything goes just the way I want it to — my way — where I am the boss and your "beautiful" cell becomes my servant.
Scientist:	(*disgusted*) You make me sick.
Virus:	Ah! That is what I enjoy most!

Both the above skit and questions can be used within the regular classroom as the instructional part of the lesson. They are then followed by differentiated activities.

One way of differentiating the activities of the gifted and other student who have clearly mastered the content is to cluster group these students. Then ask them to brainstorm a variety of answers to the last two questions listed above. After choosing some of the best brainstormed ideas, students use these chosen ideas as a springboard for an independent study project. An additional method of generating ideas for projects would be to challenge the students to find as many different ways of gathering and presenting information about viruses as possible.

Once the students have generated many ideas, let them choose one of their ideas for further development. Ask them to set goals for an independent study project and develop a feasible time-line. Students should then submit both for the teacher's approval.

During this time, students lacking mastery of the content work on materials that re-teach, review, and reinforce the information presented in the skits.

One easy way to efficiently differentiate the curriculum for the gifted within the regular classroom is to follow the discussion with a variety of activities of varying difficulty levels. Students work on activities with a difficulty level appropriate to their ability.

Students make their own virus zoo using pictures, clay models, drawings, etc. The goal of this activity is to place the virus in its proper environment and describe its life style. The teacher provides the students with a list of resources to help them research their information. The primary focus of this activity is to help students master the essential content of the lesson.

Students write an article for a newspaper entitled "Yes. There are Some Useful Viruses." This topic will lead students into studying the viruses that attack harmful insects and how they are useful to various fields such as agriculture.

Teachers can upgrade this activity to meet the needs of the gifted. Ask students to prepare a debate or write an article for an agricultural digest contrasting the effectiveness of using viruses to kill harmful insects and the effectiveness of insecticides.

Pretend that the viruses had a magazine (i.e., it has a readership of viruses), and you are the executive editor of it. It is your job to keep track of new viruses that might be life threatening to other viruses. Design and write a news column in which you specify which virus(es) are effected by the new discovery. Along with your column, design an appropriate advertisement for your magazine.

During this activity, students should conduct primary research of current sources. The activity requires that they analyze and synthesize the information they find in order to present it in a coherent fashion in their column. The activity is quite effective because it allows the students to use their creativity toward producing an actual product which they share with other students. During the production of these projects, students should do their own planning and set their own time-line (to be approved by the teacher).

All of the above activities can be done in a small group setting and can be carried on relatively easily within a regular classroom setting. The main function of the teacher is to act as a facilitator and ask questions that challenge the students to dig deeper into the information with which they are working.

The most effective use of this type of curriculum is to let it replace some of the lecture/concept learning activities presently in use. Combined with an excellent lab program and discussions of current scientific issues, it could easily develop into an effective curriculum meeting the needs of all students.

Renata Otterbach is an educator/author. Among her published works is Right-Brained Activities For A Left-Brained Subject. *She now resides in Wichita Falls, Texas 76308.*

Chapter 3

Humanities

Be A Capitalist In Jolly Old England
An Exciting Activity For The World History Class

By Anna Jean Seibert

I am lucky enough to offer the gifted and talented students at my high school a two hour block of World History and World Literature. This class offers a wonderful opportunity for all involved to make connections among different disciplines.

One unit I developed for this class is called "Discovery and Divine Right." As part of this unit, we discuss and read about the events in Europe and the Americas during the fifteenth through the seventeenth centuries. We talk about the voyages of discovery, the economic revolution that resulted, and the absolute monarchies that arose in Europe.

To help motivate my students to explore some of the economic issues involved in this unit, I developed the following activity. I divide the class into small groups and hand them the "Be a Capitalist in Jolly Old England in the Year of 1600" handout (p. 39). This handout offers a number of economic ventures from which my students can choose.

I assign each student in a group the job of convincing his or her group to invest their money in one of the five ventures. The students representing the various ventures then take a few minutes to research pertinent information in any of the materials available to them (i.e., textbooks, selected library books, and class notes). For example, the spokesperson for the Sir Francis Drake Trading Company discovered that Sir Francis Drake had died three years earlier, and the company was existing on his famous name. This knowledge forced the spokesperson to generate some new selling points for the company.

After the groups hear the various presentations from their members, they individually choose how to invest their money. When everyone has written how they wish to invest, I read off a yearly stock-holder report for each company. I base these reports on as many factual details as possible, but I also include some not-so-factual details and humorous notes as well. Of course, the report includes the return per share. They can then figure out how much they made or lost.

This activity offers students a motivational way to research and consider some of the economic issues involved in the this period. The group interaction and the idea of "making a fortune" makes this a fun and productive day for my young investors.

Anna Jean Seibert teaches English and history at Desoto High School, Desoto, Texas 75115.

Be A Capitalist In Jolly Old England In The Year 1600—Handout

In his will, your uncle has left you £100.00 and his collection of bugs (the latter is relatively worthless, but he hated to throw away that sack of dead bugs—your uncle was a little odd). In his will your uncle states that you must invest the entire £100.00 or lose it. Choose how you will invest this money based on the information below and any other information that you can gain from the presentations you will hear.

1. Shares of the Kings Men's Acting Company: shares sell for £2.00— last year's return was £5.00 per share.

2. The Sir Francis Drake Trading Company: shares are selling for £100.00 per share—last year's return was £1,000.00 per share.

3. Lloyds of London Insurance Company: shares are going for £10.00 per share—last year's return was £50.00 per share.

4. The Noah's Ark Shipbuilding Company: shares sell for £5.00 a share—last year's return was £20.00 per share.

5. Gourmet Coffee, Chocolate, and Eastern Exports Shoppe: shares sell for £2.00—this is a new venture.

Write down how you want to invest your money. In addition to the information above and gained from presentations, take into consideration all of the information we have discussed and read about this period. At the end of the class, I will let you know how your investments did.

Conflicts In Values
Activities That Involve Students
With Young Adult Literature

By Nancy Polette & Gloria Lavine

In the Winter 1991 issue of The Prufrock Journal, *Susan Giddings offered readers sound reasons for encouraging gifted students to read young-adult literature. In order to explore this subject further, we asked Nancy Polette and Gloria Levine, well-known educational authors, to provide some successful activities to encourage student involvement with young-adult literature. The following article is their kind response to our request.* — ed.

"Conflicts in Values" was written for the dual purpose of promoting critical thinking about values and motivating students to read books in which characters deal with confusion about the nature of their own ideas. Thus, the activities encourage students to define what they value, to consider alternative beliefs, and to examine possible decision-making strategies for coping with confusion about disparate choices confronting them. The suggested readings have been chosen from among books for young adults written about characters with whom most young people can identify personally or recognize in peers. The characters deal with values in such areas as family, friendships, religion, school, clothing, and rules.

Warm-up activities have been included for whole-group introduction to the types of creative thinking students will be using later in small groups or independently. It is suggested that students be allowed frequently to collaborate in doing the activities and to share finished products. Such interchange is often the impetus for further creative thought. As students share ideas about the dilemmas young people confront in today's world, they become better equipped to make responsible choices. While it is not necessary to have read the books in order to do the activities, students working together generate the enthusiasm that often brings them together with the books related to their concerns.

Warm-Up Activities
For Critical Thinking

Activity 1—Fluency
The Ability To Produce Many Responses

A. Think about the many decisions that you must make in a typical day. List as many as you can.
B. Some of the decisions may be easily made; others may be problematic. Next to the difficult decisions, list as many problems associated with each as you can.
C. Consider the disagreements you have with your parents. List as many areas of disagreement as you can.
D. Consider the disagreements you have with your peers. List as many areas of disagreement as you can.

Activity 2—Flexibility
The Ability To Respond In A Variety Of Areas

A. In doing Activity 1, you have used discussion as a technique for communicating about values conflicts with classmates. Think of the many other ways artists, writers, and musicians express the conflicts in values that they perceive in the world around them. List the art form (e.g., rock music) and at least one specific example (e.g., song title) for each.
B. Look at the list of forms of art, writing, and music you made for Activity 2(A). Have you considered some of the conflicts in beliefs experienced by individuals from cultures other than yours? Can you think of works that illustrate the artists' anticipation of future values conflicts? Have you seen, read, or heard about values conflicts that occurred in the past?
C. Examine the areas of disagreement with parents you listed in Activity 1(C) and think about how you deal with these areas of conflict. Then categorize that area of values conflicts into at least three sub-categories of "handling conflict."
D. Think about how you handle disagreements with friends. Then categorize the areas of disagreement you listed in Activity 1(D) according to how you react to these disagreements. Compare your categories with the ones you used to describe handling conflict with parents. How would your classifications for "handling conflict" change if you were describing your "ideal" rather than "real" self?

Activity 3—Originality
Thinking Of New And Unique Responses

A. Buddy wants to impress rich Skye Pennington, so he takes her to
    meet his grandfather, a wealthy German. He is horrified to hear
    rumors that his grandfather's past contains dark secrets. What
    dreadful significance could his grandfather's former name,
    "Gentlehands," hold? (Read *Gentlehands*, by M.E. Kerr, Harper
    and Row, 1978).

B. Before the experimental brain operation, doctors give several psy-
    chological tests to 32-year-old Charlie, who has been retarded since
    birth. When a doctor asks Charlie what he sees when shown a
    Rorschach inkblot, Charlie cannot imagine anything. Create your
    own inkblot by dripping some black ink or porter paint onto a piece
    of white paper and folding once. When you open up the paper, what
    do you see? (Read *Flowers for Algernon*, by Daniel Keyes,
    Harcourt, Brace, Jovanovich, 1966).

C. In *Blinded by the Light* (by Robin Brancato, Knopf, 1978), a young
    man's mother and father plan to have him kidnapped. Why would
    parents do such a thing?

D. In *The Late Great Me* (by Sandra Scoppettone, G.P. Putnam's Sons,
    1976), a 17-year-old meets her boyfriend's mother for the first time
    and is shocked by her appearance. Imagine an unconventional
    location for such an introductory meeting, and describe how the
    mother might look.

Activity 4—Elaboration
Adding To Basic Ideas

A. Suppose that hearing about *The Light in the Forest* (by Conrad
    Richter, Knopf, 1966) piques your curiosity about real-life
    instances of white children kidnapped and raised by Indian fami-
    lies during frontier days. What sources might you consult to learn
    about the motivations behind such kidnapings? Where might you
    find some first hand accounts (letters, journal entries, etc.)? How
    might you find statistics showing what happened to most of the
    children when they grew to adulthood?

B. In *Lord Jim* (by Joseph Conrad, London, 1900), Jim seeks refuge
    among the "Malays," as these Pacific Islanders were known in the
    late 1800s. He falls in love with a dark-eyed beauty who is des-
    perate to know his secret. Elaborate upon the physical features
    and dress you imagine the girl, "Jewel" to have. How would you

find the present-day name and location of her homeland? Where might you find some photographs or paintings of her real-life counterparts (natives of this area)?

Activity 5—Problem Solving
Identifying A Problem, Examining Several Alternatives
For A Solution, And Arriving At A Result That Meets
Established Criteria

A. When you go to visit your grandmother in a nursing home, she
    mistakes you for her long-dead husband, and she begs your for-
    giveness for an argument she had with your grandfather before
    he died. You don't want to deceive your grandmother, you don't
    want to hurt her, and you don't want to be in this antiseptic place.
    What are the various things your might say and do? What are the
    pros and cons of each? Whose feelings do you think should take top
    priority? How would you confront this problematic situation?
    (Read "The Moustache," from a collection by Robert Cormier, *8
    Plus 1*, Pantheon, 1980).
B. You discover that one of your co-workers at a bakery is cheating
    the boss by pocketing money on several sales. The boss hired you
    when many employers would not; he has also been good to your
    co-worker, who depends on the job to support his large family. In
    addition, your co-worker has been a friend to you, defending you
    against teasing by others at the bakery. What are the various
    courses of action you could take? What are the positive and nega-
    tive ramifications of each? What do you suppose most people would
    do? What do you think you would do? (Read *Flowers for Algernon*,
    by Daniel Keys, Harcourt, Brace, Jovanovich, 1966).
C. You are a high school junior who meets a girl from a wealthy family
    that vacations each summer in your community on Long Island. You
    are elated when she goes on a date with you, but your working class
    family feels that you have no business seeing her. Your father calls
    you a snob, strikes you for lying about your whereabouts, and forbids
    you to date for two weeks. The girl, who fills your thoughts, calls and
    tells you she will pick you up. You're not only grounded, but you've
    promised to go clamming with your lonely younger brother. What are
    your choices? What will you do? Why? Predict who will be affected by
    your decision and how they will be affected. (Read *Gentlehands*, by
    M.E. Kerr, Harper and Row, 1978).

Worksheet Activity 1
Blinded By The Light

Forced Relationships

Although we should often examine either-or distinctions for the subtle possibilities being excluded, there are often times when we must choose between two possible alternatives. For example, while we should be wary of political advertisements claiming that one candidate is a saint and the other a villain, at the voting booth, we choose the one we feel is more competent to fill the post.

For each of the following, indicate which of the two choices best describes you.

1. If I were approached in a cafe by conservatively-dressed members of a cult, I would probably be more _____ than _____ (polite, impolite).
2. I would rather eat at a _____ than a _____ (natural foods restaurant with live guitar, pizza place with a juke box).
3. I am more worried that _____ than that _____ (I will do something that might upset my parents, my parents will find out that I have done something that upsets them).
4. It is more important to make my _____ than my _____ happy (parents, boy/girlfriend).
5. I prefer _____ over _____ on pizza (mushrooms, pepperoni).
6. At the pool, I am more likely to _____ (sit on the edge, push in someone who is sitting on the edge).
7. If my brother had joined a cult and broken contact with me, I would be more likely to _____ (pretend an interest in the cult so that I could find him, let my parents hire someone to find him and bring him home).
8. If I had a midterm exam tomorrow, I would be more likely to tell my boy/girlfriend _____ (that I had to study, that I would spend time with him/her).
9. If I were to oversleep and miss an important test, I would be more likely to _____ (leave a message for my teacher that a close relative had died, find my teacher and try to reschedule the test).
10. If I were to see my brother again for the first time since he had joined a cult, I would _____ (say nothing, confront him) about how uncomfortable I am about his new habit of calling me "little one" and his failure to ask about the rest of the family.

Now that you have been forced to choose between only two alternatives, return to each statement and discuss a third alternative that best describes your probable behavior. Offer an explanation for or the reasons for the actions you might choose.

Many of the dilemmas from this activity are taken from the book *Blinded by the Light*, by Robin Brancato, knopt, 1978). You may be interested in reading this book.

Worksheet Activity 2
The Contender

Would You Rather ...

Rank order each of the following alternatives, adding and ranking at least one alternative of your own for each.

Which would you rather be?
1. _____ a Black living in Harlem
   _____ a Black living in the rural midwest
   _____ a Black living in South Africa

   _____ _____

2. _____ a drug addict, sometimes numb to the ugliness of the ghetto
   _____ a member of a gang, thereby under protection from attack by its members
   _____ a Black high school drop-out scorned by other Blacks for working a menial job at a white-owned store

   _____ _____

   You have decided to become a boxer. You train hard, and prove your potential by winning your first two fights, but you realize that you don't like hurting other fighters. Your trainer, whom you admire and trust, tells you that you just don't have the killer instinct and should quit now before being hurt because, from now on, you will be matched with more experienced boxers. Would you rather...

3. _____ continue fighting, in the hope that you could become so skilled that you could win without really injuring your opponent
   _____ plan to quit, but risk injury in one last fight, so that you will know for sure whether you have made the right choice
   _____ quit now, never having lost a fight, never seriously having hurt another, and never having been seriously hurt

Now that you have been forced to choose a few alternatives, return to you ranking lists and describe other options which might be available. Many of the choices from this activity are taken from the book *The Contender,* by Robert Lipsyte, Harper and Row, 1967. You may be interested in reading this book.

Worksheet Activity 3
Light In The Forest
Summer Of My German Soldier
The Contender

Moral Dilemmas

Imagine that you are a 17-year-old who was captured by the Delaware Indians when you were five. You have been raised by them since that time, and have recently been returned against your will to your white parents. You run away and return to your tribe, to find that they plan to avenge the murder of one of your tribe by colonists, among whom are your blood family members. Tribal leaders want to use you as a decoy to lure a boatload of men and children into an ambush. How would you feel?

_____

_____

_____

_____

_____

_____

What are at least three choices you have?

_____

_____

_____

What would be the consequences of each?

_____

_____

Imagine that you are a 12-year-old Jewish girl living near a prisoner of war camp during World War II. Your father beats you and you feel that the only friend you have is Anton, the German POW you are helping to hide. If you had to sacrifice the man who had sheltered you all your life or the one you are now giving shelter, which would it be?

Imagine that you are a boy living in a New York ghetto. A boy, who was formerly your best friend, and is now a drug addict, has broken into the store where you work. He escaped through the front window, but was badly cut. You are fairly certain he is hiding in the cave in which you two played as children. What are your alternatives?

Which alternative would by best for both him and you, and explain how it would benefit the two of you?

Many of the dilemmas from this activity are taken from the books *The Light in the Forest*, by Conrad Richter, Knopf, 1953; *Summer of My German Soldier*, by Bette Greene, Dial Press, 1973; and *The Contender*, by Robert Lispyte, Harper and Row, 1967. You may be interested in reading these books.

Nurturing Gifted Writers
Ideas From A Model Program
That Fosters The Talents Of Young Authors

By Barbara M. Peisker

When we hung our shingle reading *Write Here* over the door at the Elk Grove High School Writing Center in August 1989, we wanted our students to interpret the sign literally. We anticipated *Write Here* to be a place where students with poor writing skills could seek help and learn to write. We did not foresee one of the most exciting benefits of the center. *Writer Here* acts as a catalyst for nurturing our gifted writers not only in the center, but throughout the school. To do this, the center's staff designed many interesting and creative projects. Some of our projects have been so successful that we wanted to share them.

Across-the-curriculum writing projects have been our most successful way to nurture large numbers of good writers and keep them tuned into the writing center. Elk Grove High School students are grouped—we offer advanced classes in history, biology, math and English. The writing center staff plays a major role in working with classroom teachers to create writing assignments that stimulate the imagination of young gifted writers. The assignments result from the combined efforts of both the classroom teacher and the writing center advisors. A few examples of the kinds of assignments that the writing center launches are described below. The writing center supports students with ideas for organizing and elaborating on their across-the-curriculum assignments.

A Social Studies teacher, Jim Brown, assigned his students to write an account of history from the perspective of an immigrant who was living in Chicago sometime between 1870 to 1929. Each student created a persona who would be living in Chicago and then had to write letters and/or journals from that person's perspective. The journals or letters had to concentrate on historical events including the Chicago fire, the Hay Market Affair, the Chicago's World's Exposition, the Pullman Strike, the Chicago Stockyards using Upton Sinclair's *The Jungle*; and other historic happenings during this era.

Lou Schairer, the honors biology teacher worked closely with Jane Fraser, an advisor for *Write Here*, in collaborating on an environmental issues paper for the freshman honors biology class. Students researched a specific issue regarding problem areas of our environment, with an eye to determining how they might transform the material that they read into a dialogue between two interested parties. One student, Matt Legg, researched the topic of Yellowstone after the 1989 forest fires. He used the information to create a dialogue between a forest ranger and a tourist family visiting the park. He developed his up-to-date information into an interesting paper with a creative twist.

A geography teacher Bob Koralik, with the assistance of this center staff member, created an imaginary trip somewhere in the United States, with students planning a personal itinerary. After plotting out where they would travel and what they would see, the students were then to write letters back to the teacher informing him about their trip. The students had to choose places that they had never seen and then describe them through what they found in the research. The library staff helped students research their routes with travel guidebooks and atlases.

Offering students ways to write across the curriculum is an exciting part of our program. To increase the audience of these assignments and other works, we created ways students could share their writing with others. No writer wants to communicate with a limited, one-person audience—the teacher. All students need recognition for work well done. Writing is such a painstaking process from its inception to its completion that it would certainly be foolish not to share successful manuscripts with others.

Write Here implements plans to recognize excellence in writing. Two of the most popular plans revolve around the center itself. At the beginning of the school year, John Bottigilieri, a part-time writing staff member who displays artistic flair, designed a room divider that would serve as a display area. We decorated the slanted, A-frame boards with green and gold school-color folders. Our "logo-man" perches on top of the board calling attention to the papers it displays. Student works representing the best of each class are displayed for two months in this showcase.

A second showcase for talented writers is changed each month proclaiming, "The Writer of the Month" for Elk Grove. This glass-covered area holds the first page of several essays, poems or short stories. The complete manuscript of this writer are also housed on the display board in the center.

Publishing student writing has always existed at Elk Grove, but the focus has altered with the birth of the writing center. A literary magazine entitled *e.g.* (the initials of our school, but also the Latin abbreviation for *exempli gratia*, for example) is published each year to showcase excellent works in expository and creative writing. Supplementing that publication is a second district volume representing the talented and gifted program. Each student writer may submit one favorite work. Selected works are published in a district volume entitled, *Taglines*.

The local community college has its own publication of winners of their writing contest. Winners in each category of short story, essay, poetry and drama are invited to a luncheon and then given a special publication of the winning students' works.

Our local newspaper, *The Herald,* holds an annual writing contest, and winners of poetry and short story events have their works published in the Sunday edition each year. For student writers looking for a larger audience, we encourage them to submit manuscripts to publications devoted to publishing the work of young writers (see "Publishers of Works by Young Writers").

An extra-curricular creative writing club known as "Write-On" publishes student works two or three times each year in its newsletter, *Write-On News*. Although this may not be as prestigious as the other two publications, the members of the organization enjoy having their works for others to read for pure entertainment purposes. Talented writers enjoy an audience, no matter how limited.

Finally, *Write Here* sponsors a writing contest for seniors each spring to emphasize and recognize the importance of good writing. On a designated school day, an impromptu topic in each category of essay and short fiction is placed in the hands of the willing contestants. After considering the topic in each area, the participating students assemble in the high school library. For the last three periods of the school day, they write either an essay or short story. The manuscripts are collected and judged by a panel of teachers who read the unnamed manuscripts independently. On Honors Day one winner in each category is presented with a plaque and a monetary honorarium. Local businesses financially support the contest while the writing center organizes and supplies the publicity surrounding this writing event.

Overall, *Write Here* is not unlike other high school writing centers that are burgeoning across the country (Farrell 1989). Writing centers can and, indeed, do work to develop a better community of writers, with the writing center acting as the catalyst giving student writers motivation and assistance. Supporting the writing center is a core of some thirty honor students who were invited to become tutors based on the talent they displayed in Advanced Expository Writing or similar writing classes. Our tutors volunteer time each day to spend helping others in the process of writing. Some apply for one-half credit in independent study; others will tutor merely as a learning experience. Along with teaching others how to write, they gain mastery in the technical aspects of writing. They realize that the best way to learn something is to teach it to another. The very act of trying to explain a concept to a learner gives the instructor a strong motivation to learn as much as he can. One talented tutor, Val Koval stated, "Although I sometimes feel inadequate because I'm not always correct with punctuation, I know that tutoring others will help me strengthen my own skills in writing."

Coaching writing establishes a bonding among writers. The community feeling of "we're in this together" accelerates the unifying force of tutors with their peers. Steve Rotter expressed that concept with this example. "Jenny was writing a pretty good paper, and I just helped out a little. I felt that I wasn't doing much at all. But she expressed more appreciation than I expected."

Sunil Ahuja, in discussing his personal problems learning English as a second language, identifies with the International students when he stated, "I didn't feel like writing or thinking about writing because it made me feel that everyone would laugh at me ... Now, I correct papers that were just like mine when I used to make so many mistakes, and I feel very blue when I see the same mistakes that I used to make. At the same time, I feel exhilarated that I am helping someone who wants to be helped."

The writing center does balance task and maintenance activities along with teaching the skills of writing. Students need trusting relationships so they can serve as an audience for one another, and so they will want to write for each other. The special sort of trust necessary for sharing serious writing is developed in important ways through maintenance activity—personal talk, laughter, learning about one another's backgrounds and experiences. (Zemelman & Daniels, 1988) We think *Write Here* offers an atmosphere conducive to learning, to writing, and to nurturing students.

Magazines That Publish Student Work

Creative Kids—The National Voice for Kids
P.O. Box 8813
Waco, TX 76714
Ages 8-14

The Concord Review
A Quarterly Review of Essays
by Students of History
P.O. Box 661
Concord, Massachusetts
Ages 9-12

Merlyn's Pen
The National Magazine
for Student Writing
P.O. Box 1058
East Greenwich, Rhode Island 02818
Grades 7-10

Prism
A Magazine by and for
the Gifted and Talented
P.O. Box 030464
Fort Lauderdale, Florida 33303
All Ages

Stone Soup
The Magazine by Children
P.O. Box 83
Santa Cruz, California 95063
Grades 3-7

Young Authors Magazine
The Journal for Special,
Gifted, and Talented Young Writers
3015 Woodsdale Boulevard
Lincoln, Nebraska 68502
Ages 7-18

Children's Album
P.O. Box 6086
Concord, California 94524
Ages 8-16

The Louisville Review
315 Bingham Humanities
Louisville, Kentucky 40292
Grades K-12

Shoe Tree
The Literary Magazine
by and for Young Writers
215 Valle del Sol Drive
Santa Fe, New Mexico 87501
Ages K-7

Works Cited

Farrell, P.B. (ed.) (1989).*The high school writing center*. Urbana: National Council of Teachers of English.

Zemelman, S. & Daniels, H. (1988). *A community of writers*. Portsmouth: Heinemann Educational Books, Inc.

Barbara Peisker teaches Creative Writing and is advisor to the literary magazine, e.g. in Township High School District 214 at Elk Grove High School. Jane Fraser and Barbara Peisker were involved in opening the writing center in 1989. Ms. Peisker wishes to thank her colleague, Jane Fraser, for her assistance and ideas in writing the preceding article.

Philosophy In The Classroom
Bring Plato's Symposium To Your Gifted Students

By Michael Cannon

Philosophy belongs in the classroom—especially the gifted class-room. To bring this important aspect of education to my students, I created an activity in which my students become philosophers in the tradition of Plato's *Symposium*. By reproducing the symposium in the classroom, students learn about philosophy as they do it.

In a symposium format, all students give serious thought to an abstract idea and then present their ideas to the class. They confront ideas different from their own, and evaluate and re-evaluate their own position and that of others.

Generally speaking, Plato's *Symposium* is an account of a dinner party given by the poet Agathon to celebrate his victory in the annual Athenian tragic poetry competition. Among the guests are Socrates, Aristophanes, Pausanius, Eryximachus, and other prominent Athenians. During the course of the meal, they agree to take turns speaking on the subject of love. Pausanius speaks of the glories and delights of human love, while Phaedrus praises love as a great god. Eryximachus, the physician, talks of love's effects upon nature. Aristophanes, the comic playwright, tells a fable—an intriguing tale of the circle people. Agathon, as befits the poet, gives a lyric picture of the raptures that love provides. Finally, Socrates speaks, and the discussion soars to the heights of intellectual and spiritual love. The consideration of love moves from human to the divine, from the seen beauty in people to the unseen beauty of the soul, and finally to the abstract idea of Beauty itself. The assembly is brought down to earth by the drunken arrival of Alcibiades whose praise of Socrates ends the dinner.

Before presenting this activity to your students, I strongly urge you to read Plato's *Symposium*. I have found Michael Joyce's translation (Plato, 1982) of the *Symposium* to be excellent. John Tkach (1988) has written an interesting article on Socrates that makes good background reading for you and your students. For a complete treatment of Socratic and Platonic philosophy, you will find the works of Fredrick Copleston (1946) to be excellent resources.

After familiarizing yourself with the *Symposium*, you need to give your students an introduction to the work, its characters, and general focus. Also, offer students an overview of their classroom symposium.

Once your students have some background information, elicit a definition of the term "abstract." After the class is comfortable with the concept, ask for examples of abstract ideas as possible topics for the class symposium. Friendship, honesty, truth, and death are often topics suggested by students experienced in the symposium format. Beware of topics that are not really abstract. Students new to the concept often mention forms of popular music or such topics as dating. When something too specific is suggested, ask the student to speculate as to what larger category their suggestion could be assigned. After several good topics have been listed, have students vote to choose the one idea that they feel has the most possibilities for exploration and discussion.

After your students choose a topic, it may be advisable for them to do some background reading. If love or a related topic is chosen, you may want students to read the entire *Symposium* in preparation. Other Platonic dialogues investigate different abstract concepts. *Lysis* is concerned with friendship, *Laches* with courage, and *Phaedo* with death and immortality. *Timeaus* focuses on cosmology, the study of the structure of the universe, but the dialogue is also interesting in that it presents ideas in the form of a myth. Students may want to consider this story as a possible format for their own presentations.

Next, students prepare a speech or other presentation based on the topic chosen by the class. As in the *Symposium*, the presentations may take many forms. Speeches, poems, songs, stories, and fables are all acceptable. There are no inherent limits to the kind of presentations that students may prepare. Speeches are the most often used form, and I encourage students to use an informative or persuasive composition format when planning their speeches. When one class used friendship for a topic, several students coordinated their effort. Each of their presentations began, "Real friendship is ..." Through speeches, rap songs, fables, and other presentation forms they explored the many facets of friendship.

While students may give their presentations jointly, it is important that they compose their own contribution. Originality and excellence are essential in the presentations. Encourage students to think about the topic, explore their own feelings about it, and then develop a presentation that puts an interesting new slant on it. Explain that you are looking for ideas and presentations that are really unique.

Ask students to write out their presentations beforehand. This forces them to think with pen (or keyboard) in hand. The act of writing presentations in advance encourages them to take time to think through their ideas more carefully. You may also want to use these written notes for later review.

Setting criteria for evaluation of the presentations is very important. Involve students in the creation of the criteria by which their products will be evaluated. Ask them to describe the various qualities of a good presentation. List all suggestions on the board without question or comment. In groups, the students then rank their ideas in order of importance. The groups then present their results to the entire class. After a general discussion, have the class come to a consensus.

The criteria generated by the students can then be added to a set of non-negotiable criteria which you feel should be included on the list. For example, if the students' generated criteria do not include originality of thought or extensive elaboration upon a concept, you may wish to add these to the list.

You may want to decide upon a weight for each criterion on the list either yourself or through class discussion and consensus. Regardless of the manner in which the matter is decided, be sure that everyone understands both the criteria for a good presentation and the grading procedure to be used. If you videotape the presentations, you may model the evaluation of a presentation using presentations from past years.

Your role during the symposium is demanding but essential. You must be sure that every student participates fully and that every student remains courteous. You must also respond positively to each presentation and encourage meaningful responses from other students. Ask listeners to summarize the last speaker and to state what the speaker's ideas have in common with their own ideas. If students feel compelled to disagree with a speaker, remind them to do so in a scholarly manner. The disagreements are one of the best and most stimulating parts of the symposium. In fact, you may decide to generate a bit of dissension if things get a bit dull.

At times during the symposium, you may want to question speakers closely, forcing them to see the consequences of their ideas. You can do this in a number of ways. Ask presenters to explain just what is meant by a particular word or phrase. Or, ask students to extend their thinking by asking questions such as, "If what you say is true, then what if ... ?"

It is essential that you, as leader, do not inflict your own ideas on the discussion. In fact, it is often best if the students have no idea how you feel about the ideas presented. Paraphrase a student's ideas for clarification, but do not lead them by explaining what you consider to be a "proper" interpretation of an idea. Remember that you are the facilitator of an exciting exchange, not the director of correct thinking.

The discussions will be spirited and may lead to strange conclusions. As you will notice in Plato's dialogues, rarely does this kind of discussion come to a conclusion with which everyone will agree. Ask

different students to try to find some common threads in some presentations, or to classify the presentations in categories. Another way
to close a symposium is to ask individuals what they still do not understand about the topic.

After one experience with a symposium, students usually clamor
for more. They truly enjoy the free exchange of ideas.

Works Cited

Copleston, F. (1946). *A history of philosophy*. Mahwah: Paulist Press.
Plato. (1982). *The collected dialogues*. Ed. Edith Hamilton and
    Huntington Cairns. Prinston: Bollingen.
Tkach, J.R. (1988). "Great mentor series: the philosophers Socrates,
    Plato, and Aristotle." *Challenge*. 31: 45-48.

*Michael Cannon has taught secondary students for eighteen years. He
currently teachers sixth and eighth grade gifted students at Bassett
Middle School, El Paso, Texas 79930.*

Primary Research And The Traditional Hero
An Effective Method For Teaching
Interdisciplinary Research, Thinking, and Writing

By Penny Whytlaw

What do the New Kids on the Block, Michael Jordan, pioneers, Beth March, Anne Sullivan, and Franklin Roosevelt all have in common? I know one thing they have in common—each is a personal hero of someone living in Odessa, Texas.

Heroes and heroic deeds recur throughout literature and life. This makes these concepts very appropriate for a thematic, interdisciplinary English/history unit. Since adolescents have strong feelings about their own heroes, our seventh graders enjoyed making comparisons between literary heroes and Texas heroes. But when taught in a traditional manner, our G/T students missed the important connection between history, literature, and "real" life. The following approach allows our students to make this important connection. It makes the students responsible for the entire learning process, leads them to a variety of differentiated and highly appropriate activities for G/T students, and introduces them to the principles of scholarly research and statistical reporting.

We developed these specific guidelines for a program containing a two-hour English/history block, but other buildings in our system with different scheduling demands have adapted them to meet their needs. Because of the complexity of the skills involved, we have found that this unit works best near the end of the school year. Many other activities go on concurrently, but the core of the differentiated unit is a discovery process during which students decide what they want to know about "real" heroes, use primary research skills to answer their questions, and draw conclusions about the results.

The following list overviews the process
- Brainstorm characteristics of heroes
- Develop a workable survey based on age group criteria
- Practice primary research skills through interviews
- Tabulate results
- Compile information
- Graph quantifiable results
- Draw conclusions
- Present results orally

To introduce the unit, the students brainstorm the characteristics of a hero, keeping all responses in a writer's notebook for future use during oral discussions. The list also serves as prewriting.

Next, the students develop a workable survey dealing with heroes. Using Reporter's Formula (Cowan, 1983) the students devise their own questions, four of which must be appropriate for figuring percentages (i.e., quantifiable). After the students come to a consensus about the questions, a survey sheet is prepared.

For example, students might generated such questions as "Who is/was your hero(es) or heroin(es) and why?" "What are the characteristics of your hero/heroine?" "Has your hero/heroine ever been disliked? If so, why?" "Do other people see your hero/heroine the way you do?" "As your life has changed, has your choice of a hero/heroine changed?"

The students interview people outside the class and record the responses to the interview questions. We have learned that the only variable that greatly influences the results is the age of the person being interviewed, but the students must discover this conclusion for themselves.

The students have five days to complete their surveys. (Yes, weekends count.) The day the students turn in their surveys, we check them to see that information has been recorded under each question, and that each student has interviewed one person from each of the required age groups. (Following directions = 100!)

The next day we return the surveys to their owners, putting history and English classes together to tabulate results. Results of the surveys can be tabulated in various ways, most of which result in students learning nothing and teachers staying up all night. The following step-by-step group technique, developed by my history teacher counterpart, works well for us. It also enhances the students "ownership" of the unit.

We place the students in small groups according to the number of age groups (six age groups with six students in each student group) and give them clean survey sheets. Each student is responsible for recording information for one age group. They pass around the survey sheets containing the original interviews, record the information pertaining only to their assigned age group on the clean survey sheet, initial the original interview sheet, and pass it on to other small group members.

When the small groups finish recording information, we put them into larger groups—made up according to age groups. We put all students responsible for the same age group together. This new group has information about only one age group. The students then compile their information about that age group and graph this information, using different kinds of graphs (bar graphs, pie graphs, tally sheets, etc.) for each of the four quantifiable questions in the survey.

We give each group one clean transparency and various transparency pens. The students then graph the data and record pertinent information. During the oral presentation each group must present a consensus conclusion about that particular age group based on the data.

Before any class discussion takes place, the students must draw whatever over-all conclusions they can from the data and record this in their writer's notebooks. Following this, an open-ended discussion results, after which the students are given time for written response.

The process of tabulating, compiling, reporting, discussion, and responding generally takes two full days of our two-hour block. But it is time well spent.

Regular classroom activities take place before, during, and after the survey with as much tie-in to the theme as possible. Every journal entry, reading-writing connection, literature reading, and oral discussion deals in some way with the theme. All of these activities lead up to the final event of the year—a product generated by the many ideas bursting from the notebooks and minds of the students.

By using this approach, the students come up with many new connections. They become interested in further research, and they even learn that many "real" heroes are found on the pages of books. I can't wait until I teach this unit again when I might find out that The New Kids on the Block, Michael Jordan, pioneers, Beth March, Anne Sullivan, and Franklin Roosevelt have much more in common than I know.

Works Cited

Cowan, Elizabeth. *Writing*. Glenview: Scott Foresman, 1983.

Penny Whytlaw teaches English at Bonham Junior High School, Odessa, Texas 79762. Ms. Whytlaw thanks Vicki Leach, Ector County ISD, and Lucinda Windsor and Susie Whitsell, Midland ISD, for their help and ideas in writing the preceding article.

Read Me, Please!
Young-Adult Literature—A Valuable Addition To Any Gifted Classroom

By Susan Giddings

When I walk into a library, books leap off the shelves, clamoring for my attention. "Read me, please!" I always find it difficult to select just one or two or three books; the many choices overwhelm me. I want to read them all! Bringing this enthusiasm for books to my students is another matter.

Last year, as I began teaching a language arts gifted and talented class, I held the belief that my students would share my love for books. However, when I told my students about all the outside reading they would be doing, they were not overly enthusiastic.

One student expressed the majority opinion, "More Reading? When are we going to have time to read? We have too much homework as it is. I don't want to waste my time reading even more." Their attitude devastated me. Reading, a waste of time? How could these extremely bright students feel this way?

Unfortunately, the majority of American students share the opinion of my class. A recent newspaper article stated that eighth-grade students spend an average of 1.8 hours a week on outside reading ("What eighth-graders do with their time," 1990). That translates to approximately 17 minutes a day of reading for pleasure.

Furthermore, the state of reading in our society in general is in decline. Will and Winglee (1990) report that only 7 to 12 percent of the adult population reads any form of serious contemporary literature during the course of a year. And, 44 percent of the adult population are self-proclaimed non-readers.

Surely my gifted eighth-graders offered exceptions to such grim figures. Imagine my disappointment when the majority of my students agreed that they spend little more time reading than the average eighth grader in the newspaper article. Although several said they would like to read more, most students put pleasure reading relatively low on their list of priorities.

Yet, in truth, reading ought to be high on that list. With the renewed fervor for thinking skills and increasing concern over dropping SAT scores, educators, students, and parents must make reading and its many benefits an educational priority. To become a nation of thinkers, we must become a nation of readers. The benefits of reading are numerous. Increased vocabulary, improved comprehension and word attack skills, better insight into contemporary issues, and a greater awareness of individual differences are but a few. Our students, especially gifted and talented students, need to return to reading.

Although many gifted students are voracious readers early in school, during junior high or middle school their interest wanes. Students often complain that assigned readings are boring and other books are not interesting or relevant. For this reason, book reports tend to be dry, dull re-tellings of a plot or creative plagiarism of a book flap.

Providing students with a reading list containing high interest, relevant adolescent literature may alleviate this problem. Few students, gifted or non-gifted, willingly read books they perceive as boring. A reading list containing high quality young-adult literature can offer reluctant readers an exciting alternative to traditional texts.

Young-adult literature offers gifted students a type of reading quite appropriate for their needs. Susan Rakow (1991) explains, "Critically important for teachers to recognize is that many young-adult novels are well written, carefully crafted, emotionally powerful works of literature. They can be used to teach or reinforce all of the aspects of literary analysis, personal response, and introspection which are part of even the most advanced reading and writing curriculum."

Young-adult literature addresses the cognitive needs of the gifted. Baskin and Harris (1980) state, "Books should be identified for high-ability children on the basis of both intrinsic and extrinsic qualities." The most important intrinsic quality is language. The language should be, "rich, varied, accurate, precise, and exciting." Students often reject books with dated style, vocabulary, and expressions. Young adult literature offers readers vivid, vibrant language.

A complex and open-ended content and structure are two other intrinsic qualities important for high ability readers. Baskin and Harris (1980) explain that "contemplating, analyzing, and judging continuously takes place during reading and for a long time afterward." Because young-adult literature often deals with universal issues in a highly relevant context, it requires an intellectual response from the student. Students can no longer be passive readers; they must think and react to the readings.

Gifted students should be challenged intellectually and exposed to a wide variety of people and ideas (Halsted, 1988). Adolescent literature can do that too. A small town student who reads about gangs in New York or two teens living in Brazil is exposed to different people and different lifestyles.

While young-adult literature does much to meet the cognitive needs of gifted students, it may do an even better job of meeting their affective needs. Gifted students reading young-adult literature learn that the problems they face are not unique. At an age when many students feel isolated, they often find that they share many dilemmas with others through adolescent literature. They learn that they are not alone.

According to Rakow (1991), gifted students, "need young-adult books to help illuminate and validate their own experiences." Rakow goes on to say that, "Painfully aware of how their giftedness is sometimes a difference that separates them from their classmates, they can certainly share the poignant humor of the passage in S.E. Hinton's *Outsiders* (1968) when one of the Socs is teased about his 'highwater pants.' Especially during early adolescence, few students are comfortable being different."

Furthermore, the use of adolescent literature increases the degree of control gifted students have over their education. By allowing students to select an adolescent novel, I place the responsibility of choice on them. They are responsible for their reading decisions. Rather than participating in a teacher-directed activity, they are involved in a student-directed experience. They become increasingly independent learners.

Yet, students do need some guidance at first. The teacher can give this guidance by offering students a limited list of adolescent literature. Award winning books, recommended reading lists from national organizations, and recommendations from other teachers are all good places to start a search for the best titles. Later, as both the teacher and the students become more familiar with this area of literature, the list can be expanded, and individual students can contract for books not found on the list.

Such a process need not exclude the classics. In fact, by including both types of literature on a reading list, many students will discover the joy of the classics for themselves and willingly read them.

If we are to create a nation of readers, we must offer students material that is interesting and relevant. Available choices on reading lists need to shift from those which are the teachers' favorites to those preferred by students. Reading must be encouraged not discouraged; students' interests must be fostered, not allowed to fester. Trelease (1985) explains, "Reading is, among other things, a skill, and like all skills, the more you use it the better you become at it." Only when we offer students books they will read with relish will students become avid readers.

Figure 1 lists a number of books which my students enjoy. When I pass this list to students, a muttered "more reading?" may still be heard, but it is the minority opinion. Most students view the readings as fun and challenging. They realize that they are in charge of their reading material. The exposure to different characters, lifestyles, themes, and ideas has opened new concepts and questions for the students. Going to the library is no longer an arduous task but an enjoyable outing. Many students begin hearing the same refrain as I do when in the library, "Read me, please!"

Suggested Reading List

* *1984* by George Orwell. A science fiction classic that makes dire predictions for the future. 1984 coined the term "Big Brother" & "newspeak." Mature theme.
* *The Chocolate War* by Robert Cormier. Jerry refuses to succumb to peer pressure and is bullied by other students. Mature language.
* *Dicey's Song* by Cynthia Voigt. Dicey demonstrates independence and self-reliance as she takes her brothers and sisters to the grandmother they've never met.
* *Fahrenheit 451* by Ray Bradbury. All books are banned in this science fiction novel.
* *Flowers for Algernon* by Daniel Keyes. Charley, a retarded man, is given an experimental drug to boost his intelligence.
* *Interstellar Pig* by William Sleator. A board game is actually a struggle between aliens and humans. Mature theme and language.
* *The Lord of the Flies* by William Golding. In this classic story of survival, a group of boys must fend for themselves on an island. Mature theme and language.
* *Memory* by Margaret Mahy. Johnny's guilt over his sister's death suppresses his memory. His friendship with Sophie, an elderly woman suffering from Alzheimer's, helps him to remember and accept the past. Mature theme and language.
* *The Moves Make the Man* by Bruce Brooks. Jayfox, a gifted black boy, becomes friends with an emotionally disturbed boy.
* *Rebecca* by Daphne DuMaurier. In this classic tale of mystery and suspense, the narrator discovers the truth behind the death of her husband's first wife.
* *The Summer of My German Soldier* by Bette Greene. Patty, a Jewish girl, befriends a German soldier who is at a POW camp in Arkansas.

- *White Fang* by Jack London. Part dog, part wolf, White Fang fights for survival against the harshness of the North and the cruelty of his masters.
- *Wuthering Heights* by Emily Bronte. The tragic love story of Catherine and Heathcliffe is a favorite of readers.

Works Cited

Baskin, B.H. and Harris, K.H. (1980). *Books for the gifted child*. New York: R.R. Bowker Company.

Halsted, J.W. (1988) *Guiding gifted readers: from preschool to high school*. Columbus Ohio: Ohio Psychology Publishing Company.

Hinton, S.E. (1968). *The outsiders*. New York: Dell.

Rakow, S.R. (1991). Young-adult literature for honors students? *English Journal*, January, 1991, 80 (1), 48-51.

Trelease, J. (1985). *The read aloud handbook*. New York: Penguin Books.

"What eighth-graders do with their time." (1990). *Parade*. November 18, 1990, 22.

Will, N. and Winglee, M. (1990). *Who reads Literature?* Washington, D.C.: Seven Locks Press.

Susan Giddings has taught English at the secondary level for eleven years. She now teaches at Marble Falls Middle School, Marble Falls, Texas 78654.

Trends And Traditions
An Integrated Unit For The Middle School

By Alisa B. Wagner

St. Nick travels around the world ... Greek gods come to life ... King Arthur rides in gallantly ... Mother Theresa gives a heart warming speech ... These events all form a part of the gifted and talented curriculum I've developed called "Trends and Traditions."

Quite soon after beginning my first year teaching a middle school language arts class for gifted and talented students, I realized that I would have to extend my curriculum far beyond the limits of language arts. I discovered what many experts in the field of gifted education already knew: "Content of curriculum for the gifted and talented should focus on and be organized to include a more complex and in-depth study of major ideas, problems and themes that integrate knowledge with and across systems of thought" (Passow, 1982).

After a good deal of thought and preparation, I developed my "Trends and Traditions" unit. My sixth grade students find this unit to be their most enlightening, enriching, and enjoyable. Multidisciplinary in focus, this unit combines research, writing, reading, social studies, science, and math. The unit takes about 6–8 weeks and covers a wide variety of topics, interests, and subjects.

"Celebrations of Giving Around the World" comprises the first section of the "Trends and Traditions" unit. The purpose of this section is to develop an understanding and appreciation for other cultures. Almost all cultures and countries have a celebration during which gifts are exchanged. Students choose a country and research that country's celebration through giving. They then compile their research into a short summary and share the information orally with the class.

The student presentations culminate in a "Celebrations of Giving Around the World" festival. I invite parents, administrators, community leaders, and other teachers to attend this festival. Each student or student group decorates a booth for their country. They must include a minimum of three visual or kinesthetic products, and as the visitors mill around the room, the students must give a brief description of each product. Thus, they not only learn about but experience a wide array of celebration traditions.

"Greek Gods: A Passage Through Time" forms section two of my "Trends and Traditions" unit. The first part of the adventure is an experience with Greek mythology. To introduce this section, a local storyteller comes and gives her interpretation of the epic poem

Gilgamesh. In the first section of study, the students examine different literary types—fables, myths, and legends. They then research and present to the class facts in history that surround the writing of the Greek myths. Included in this research is an examination of the architecture, dress, language, general lifestyles of the Greeks, and the Trojan War. Then as a class, we overview the important Greek gods and goddesses. This includes the creation of a large family tree which shows the relationships between the various Greek deities.

Next, the students create an original myth which conforms to the characteristics of the Greek myth. Their myth must offer an explanation of a natural phenomenon not explained by other myths read by the class. Students then read their myths to the class

This section's grand finale involves a "Feast of the Gods." Students come to class dressed as and playing the parts of various Greek deities. While on this earthly spot, they enjoy ambrosia—Oreos, Nacho Cheese Doritos, and M&Ms.

Section three of the "Trends" unit is "A Visit to the Middle Ages." To begin this section of study, we view the classic film, *Camelot*. From this experience, we discuss the various aspects of music and dance found in the musical. We then move to a discussion of the speech, dress, and general lifestyles of people during the Middle Ages.

Inevitably, the discussion moves to the topic of knights. The class discusses the heroic qualities of knights. Then, as groups, the students read about chivalry, the code of honor binding the behavior of knights, and compile a modern day code of honor. They also read about the dress of the knights and create an individual coat of arms using symbols and codes to represent ideas that describe themselves. Finally, the students use the information they have gathered about life and heroes in the Middle Ages to persuade the rest of the class that either Lancelot or King Arthur was the true hero of the time. The students accomplish this in persuasive essays which are followed by a debate between the opposing sides.

The final section of the "Trends and Traditions" unit focuses on modern day heroes. This section is divided into two parts. The first part is a study of what a hero is and who our modern heroes are, and the second is an in-depth look at a single modern hero.

To begin the first part, students brainstorm and then discuss the question, "Are there any modern day heroes?" The class then compiles a list of the ideal characteristics of a hero. They also look at the classification of "Heroes" in the *Guinness Book of World Records*. Then, they evaluate their modern heroes using the characteristics which they generated.

The students next write and administer a survey focusing on the characteristics of heroes and the heroes of various populations in our society. Before doing so, the class discusses the characteristics of a valid survey and some statistical methods involved in analyzing the raw data of a survey. The students identify their target populations and develop a survey form. Finally, they conduct their survey and compile their results. These results are presented to the class. All presentations include at least one graph or chart which illustrates their findings.

During the second part of the this section, students study a modern hero in an in-depth manner. Each student chooses a personal hero and then conducts research into that individual's life. They then compile their research and create a campaign for "The Hero of the Century." As a part of the campaign, the students perform a jingle, write a slogan, make a poster and bumper sticker, produce and perform an advertisement, and give a campaign speech. The students then vote for "The Hero of the Century"—they, of course, cannot vote for their own candidate. Last year, Mother Theresa won.

Students leave this unit with a higher level of consciousness concerning the heroes, trends, and traditions that shape their world. But, most important, the students become enthusiastic about learning, discovering, and creating.

Works Cited

Passow, A. H. (1982). *Differentiated curricula for the gifted / talented: a point of view*. In Sandra Kaplan and others (eds.). *Curriculum for the Gifted*. Ventura, California: Ventura County Superintendent of Schools Office.

Alisa Wagner has taught gifted and talented students at the middle school level for two years. She is currently teaching sixth grade English at Marble Falls Middle School, Marble Falls, Texas 78654.

Creating Simulations For The History Classroom
Effective Use Of The Simulation To Teach Content

By Bruce Doolittle

O*ne major problem with history education in America is the system used to teach social studies in our schools, a system known technically, among professional educators, as the Boring Method.*
—Dave Barry from Dave Barry Slept Here

At the beginning of each school year, I make a personal commitment to avoid the Boring Method of teaching history. A role-playing simulation is one of the best tools I have for avoiding this method of education.

Role-playing simulations have long been touted as successful ways to make learning exciting and valuable for gifted students (Treffinger, 1980). I find that once students know what a role-playing exercise is all about, they tend to get more excited about what they are learning. Highly verbal students are particularly intrigued by the chance to do something other than write a research paper or take another essay exam. A well-designed simulation helps develop research skills, public speaking proficiency, and many of the cognitive skills of Bloom's Taxonomy. Using simulations in the gifted classroom can be easy and successful. In this article, I will outline a simulation procedure that has worked well for me.

The first step in setting up a role-playing exercise is to explain to the students the basic premise of the simulation, explain the goals of the simulation, and offer an overview of the sequence of events during the simulation (Treffinger, 1980). In the case of the simulation I will use as an example below, I tell my class that we will hold two U.S. Senate subcommittee hearings on topics of international concern—"The Japanese Economic Challenge" and "U.S.-Third World Relations."

I explain that these hearings will involve several students who will role-play U.S. senators and several other students who will role-play "expert witnesses" appearing before the senators. Six or seven students play senators and the rest play the roles of experts in our two-hour hearings. In large classes, remaining students role-play members of the international press corps. As journalists they observe the hearing, ask questions of the witnesses and/or senators, and write a two- or three-page news story about the event (either in the style of a wire service story or a weekly news magazine article).

I explain that the experts will appear before the senators to deliver specialized information and answer the senators' questions. But, I explain, before the experts testify, the senators will deliver short statements (approximately three to five minutes) that express their views about the topic at hand. For example, the U.S. senator from California might mention the concerns of his constituents regarding U.S. and Japanese trade.

I then explain that the experts will come forth to testify one at a time and that these experts will take 30 seconds or so to talk about themselves. It is amusing to see high school students talk with straight faces about obtaining an Ivy League doctorate in two or three years and then becoming, say, assistant secretary of state soon afterward.

The simulation is always grounded in important content, and while students have fun, they also learn the important concepts surrounding the issues with which they are dealing. In fact, students even begin to identify and understand those issues that will have the greatest impact on the future. For example, in 1987 one of my students opened the "Japanese Challenge" hearing as Senator Karsarus from Michigan and included the following remarks: "My constituents are sick and tired of the perception that Japanese cars are superior to American cars. My friends in Detroit say, and I believe them, 'What we need to do is address two problems—the problem of Japan's dumping of automobiles and other industrial products, and the problem of Japan's super-protective market.' I ask my esteemed fellow senators, how can we adequately compete with Japan when the economic playing field is uneven and the other team ignores the rules?" In 1987, this student clearly had a firm grasp of a problem that would profoundly affect our present presidential campaign.

Next, I explain that the expert witnesses will spend three or four minutes giving personal commentary on the issue at hand and suggest how the U.S. government should handle things in the future.

For example, a student role-playing Maku Chippu, a Japanese-American specialist on high technology trade between the two countries, made these opening remarks in our hearing: "The U.S. government should address the Japanese challenge in three key ways. First, the American government should provide more expert assistance to small American companies that are not sure about how to penetrate the Japanese market. Second, the U.S. government should monitor Japanese trade practices more closely than ever in order to reduce any illegal activities. Third, the U.S. government should, through the Department of Education, increase the funding for scholarships to American college students who study the Japanese language."

After each testimonial, I explain, the senators will have a chance to cross-examine the experts. Three to five questions has been an adequate number in the past, but certainly more could be asked. The fact that a role-playing exercise really tests the ability of students to think on their feet—or "seats" to be more precise—is another bonus of this activity.

Once I have explained how the simulation will work, I help my students choose their roles. If students are somewhat familiar with the controversial aspects of a particular subject, they will choose a role that tends to personify their own view. For example, if a student is troubled by rain forest destruction in the Third World, then that individual will probably jump at the chance to role-play an environmentalist who has written books and articles on the deforestation of tropical rain forests. I encourage students to create their own characters. But I have found that many students prefer to choose a role from a list of suggestions I provide. Whatever the case, I generally ask students to list their top three choices in order of preference. I collect these requests and then, after class, I make the actual role assignments.

I should mention that many students love making up aliases to go along with their roles. Students have amazed me with their ability to create clever names such as Texas Senator Frieda Turade, New York Senator I.B. D'Bigappo, and Chrysler Motors President Otto Maker. The possibilities are virtually endless.

After students have received their role-playing assignments, I meet individually with them in what I call "research conferences." In these meetings I make suggestions to the students about resources they might consult in order to prepare for their roles. This is also a good time to remind the students that I am hoping they will not merely give an oral report at the hearing, but instead will attempt to take on the persona and world-view of the person who actually lives the student's "role" in the real world. I also suggest that the students examine the customs and dress of their characters so they can really ham it up during the simulation.

This is a challenging research assignment and my assistance as a research facilitator is definitely appreciated. I think it is fair to say that the more familiar an instructor is with the literature relating to the topic of the simulation, the better.

The next step is what I call the "brainstorming step." This step is important for two reasons: it provides students with creative ideas and lowers their anxiety level. During the brainstorming step, the class generates, for each other, suggestions about sources to read, things to say, ways to dress, ways to act, and other creative touches that might be employed. The hope here is to promote a positive, supportive, and non-competitive atmosphere for the simulation.

Now, the students are ready to do research in the library. It has been a good idea in the past to meet individually with students periodically during their research in order to answer questions and to make sure that their research is coming along well, but at this point, most students have a very clear direction for their research.

Before the simulation, I like to engage students in some "verbal sparring" with one another. By this, I mean that students not only listen to each other's opening remarks and evaluate them, but pepper each other with the kind of probing questions that a discerning senator might ask at a hearing. This "dress rehearsal" activity has proven to be very beneficial for students who need to rethink portions of their prepared speeches and to continue studying the subject in more detail.

The final step, of course, is the simulation. Just before it starts, I usually remind the students to stay in character and encourage them to relax and have fun. Also, I remind the senator who is chair of the sub-committee that he or she, not I, is in control of the hearing. The hearing is a time when I sit back and watch my students perform. My main function during the simulation is to congratulate students on their performances.

Another benefit of the role-playing simulation is that it continues to help the students long after their characters are put away. In the weeks that follow, inevitably references are made to the Senate hearing by the students. The role-playing exercise becomes woven tightly into the fabric of the course curriculum.

I feel confident that if you design a Senate hearing around a complex and controversial subject such as U.S. foreign policy in Eastern Europe, acid rain legislation, or toxic waste policy, and if you foster a comfortable atmosphere for having fun and taking risks, your students will benefit significantly from such an activity. Best of all, you may never have to use the Boring Method of teaching.

Good luck and good role-playing.

Works Cited

Treffinger, D.J. (1980). *Encouraging creative learning for the gifted and talented: a handbook of methods and techniques.* Ventura: Ventura County Superintendent of Schools Office.

Bruce Doolittle presently teaches history at McCallum High School in Austin, Texas (78756).

Using Science Fiction Literature
Teaching Important Literary Ideas Using Science Fiction

By Dr. Benny Hickerson

In Ray Bradbury's classic work of science fiction, *Fahrenheit 451*, books are considered dangerous and are, therefore, destroyed on the premise that the thoughts they contain cause confusion and unhappiness; better not to think at all than to be made unhappy by thinking. How far are we today from Bradbury's world of the future, or from George Orwell's totalitarian society depicted in *1984* in which the ministry of Truth exists to lie to the people and communication is effectively reduced to the "sound bites" of Newspeak? What rich, provocative material for gifted students to examine, analyze, discuss, and debate!

Gifted students especially seem to relate to science fiction and fantasy literature, possibly because it offers so much for the creative mind and, if good, requires critical analysis and evaluation for full appreciation. Good writers of science fiction and fantasy extend the known into the future unknown, creating fantastic but plausible, even possible future events. Science fiction often contains elements of satire and irony which appeal to the gifted student's sophisticated sense of humor. Too, science fiction and fantasy literature often present social and political commentary, with moral and ethical themes that speak to the strong social sense that is characteristic of the gifted. As excellent works of science fiction and as literary classics, *Fahrenheit 451* and *1984* offer much to stimulate the minds of gifted learners.

The following activities provide opportunities for gifted learners to participate in self-directed independent learning and cooperative, group learning, and develop reading and writing skills in connection with the novels to be studied. The activities conform to many of the principles for a differentiated curriculum for the gifted outlined by Kaplan (1979), Taba (1961), and Treffinger (1980).

Fahrenheit 451

To introduce the study of *Fahrenheit 451*, divide students into three groups, appointing a chairperson and recorder in each group. Present a scenario in which all videotapes and films have been declared dangerous and banned by the government; to own or to view any film is a criminal act punishable by imprisonment. Special government agents seek out any contraband video or films and destroy them for the protection of the people. Assign each group one of the following problems for discussion:

- Why might films be considered dangerous, and for what reasons might they be outlawed by a government?
- How would people go about hiding films they wished to protect? How would the viewing equipment be hidden, and how would they go about viewing secret films?
- Should a responsible citizen, knowing that a neighbor has hidden films and viewing equipment illegally, report this criminal activity to protect the neighborhood?

The chairperson in each group is responsible for ensuring that all members have the opportunity to contribute to the discussion, while the recorder keeps notes of the discussion. From these notes, a presenter from each group will report to the entire class and conduct discussion with the class as a whole on each problem. The teacher's role is to solicit supporting reasoning for statements of opinion, asking: "Why do you think this would be likely to happen? What prior conditions would be necessary for this to occur? What would be the likely consequences of such actions?" These questions are adaptations from those suggested in Taba (1962) as aids for developing concepts and generalizations.

As students begin to read *Fahrenheit 451*, point out that the situation in the novel is parallel to the hypothetical situation they have been discussing, only it is books that have been banned. As they read, ask them to consider why certain characters in the story value books so highly and whether or not they believe this to be realistic under the circumstances of the story.

1984

While Bradbury's setting is some unspecified future time, Orwell has given his readers a specific date, and that date has now come and gone. That fact can be used to generate interest in the novel: the work represents Orwell's prediction of the future as he saw it developing at the time he wrote the novel immediately after World War II, in 1948 (he merely reversed the final two digits of the year). This can be used to set up questions to consider while reading: What were his predictions of our world today? What events may have influenced his bleak view of the future? How accurate were his predictions? How much of Orwell's vision of the future has now become reality?

Provide a brief introduction explaining the setting of the novel: the world is divided into three super-states among which there is constant conflict but ever-changing alliances; the Ministry of Truth rewrites history, altering news and magazine reports to conform with the propaganda of the government (Big Brother); two-way telescreens are in every room to monitor everyone's actions, even thoughts and feelings; posters everywhere proclaim "Big Brother is Watching You!"

As students read *1984*, they are to record on note cards the page number of any specific event, description, action, or statement that they may wish to refer to later in class discussion or in writing. Particularly, they should note any parallels they can see in the world today, examples of irony, and any terms used or invented by Orwell that they find important, interesting, or otherwise significant. They may want to briefly describe or annotate the event and/or write a brief personal reaction or comment.

At various points as students are reading the novel, allow a class period for discussion based on students' notes.

At other times, students use their creative skills to write about the arrest and interrogation of Julia and Winston from the point of view of a member of The Brotherhood or that of a minor government official reporting to O'Brien. An alternate creative writing assignment is to have students assume the roles of television news reporters covering the scene of a book burning or the arrest of Julia and Winston, and to report with as much detail and realism as possible, presenting the reports on videotape. Oral and videotape presentations allow for evaluation and immediate feedback from the class, based on the criteria of the assignment: accuracy from the point of view of the character and the story, and original and creative detail in reporting and presenting.

Students may choose to write an essay in which they compare or contrast styles of science fiction or fantasy writers, including some of those previously discussed or others with whom they are familiar. (There is great contrast between Douglas Adams' *Hitchhiker's Guide to the Galaxy* and Orwell's *1984*, for example). Some students may read Orwell's *Animal Farm* and compare the message and form of this novel with *1984*.

As always, when working with gifted students, the teacher must remain flexible and open to alternative ideas for assignments or ways in which to fulfill an assignment—often gifted students have better ideas! Keep in mind the objectives of the study: analysis of the literary genre of science fiction and of two works specifically; exploration of the themes and messages of these novels; and stimulation of critical analysis and creative thinking. To these, the teacher may add specific skills and techniques of research and essay or creative writing or oral presentation. Then, if students come in with something completely off-the-wall and unexpected, evaluate it in terms of these criteria and prepare to be delighted.

Works Cited

Kaplan, S.N. (1979) *Inservice training manual: activities for developing curriculum for the gifted / talented.* Ventura: Ventura County Superintendent of Schools Office.

Taba, H. (1962). *Curriculum development: theory and practice.* New York: Harcourt, Brace, and World.

Treffinger, D.J. (1980). *Encouraging creative learning for the gifted and talented: a handbook of methods and techniques.* Ventura: Ventura County Superintendent of Schools Office.

Benny Hickerson is currently the gifted and talented education consultant for the Hurst-Euless-Bedford Independent School District in Bedford, Texas (76022).

Creative Written Products in English
Writing For Other Audiences

By Millie Goode

Helping students develop meaningful, creative products is always a challenge for teachers of gifted students. Yet, they are important. Experts in the field of gifted education extol the virtues of having students develop products which demonstrate their mastery of content and skills (Kaplan, 1979).

The coordinator in my district conducts a "products fair" each school year. Naturally, the coordinator expects me to provide—you guessed it—products for display.

To be honest, I personally believe products to be of value, for it is through such tangible student production that I, as well as the parents, coordinators, and community, have an opportunity to witness the value of the gifted and talented program in this district.

Nevertheless, such joy and potential rewards cannot answer the question, "What products should be developed?" Helping students develop products that demonstrate that the students have mastered important skills is a challenge. In the following article, I offer one approach to teaching product development that helps students in just this way.

Writing provides an excellent vehicle for producing the "product" with which many gifted programs are concerned. Emphasis on the writing process has intensified in recent years, manifesting itself in essential elements of instruction and writing workshops for teachers. For this reason alone, written products become a focal point for gifted programs in any content area. Ward (1961) points out in *Differential Education for the Gifted* that since a strong relationship exists between language and thought, writing provides an excellent outlet for developing and clarifying thought processes. To help students begin to deal with their inner feelings, develop their writing voice and style, and learn complex concepts, initial writing needs to be expressive, reflexive, or personal. Expressive writing allows personal growth through exploration and discovery. Personal writing can involve the autobiography (focusing on the writer), memoir (focusing on someone from the past), or portrait (focusing on someone in the present).

With these factors in mind, let me describe one of my favorite products—the personal essay or story. To ensure success in this assignment, I have created the following teacher "to do" list:

- Expose the students to exceptional examples of the type of personal experience writing desired;
- Review with students products from previous years (first-year teachers can simply expand the first and fifth items on this list);
- Develop a list of alternative essay or story topics and approaches gathered from a product scope and sequence, brainstorming with the students, and/or a teacher-generated idea list;
- Develop criteria for an evaluation of the final draft of the product (which may not prevent tears of disappointment but do offer justification for grades assigned);
- Model teacher-generated examples (the best way I know of to establish teacher and product credibility and motivate the students);
- Allow students to practice and experiment with the various story ideas and methods of presentation;
- Offer feedback about the students' experimentation (mention here any items that you particularly abhor—oversized products, flimsy cover construction, liquid paper, glitter, etc.); and
- Allow students to refine their products and compose their final drafts.

The first year I used the personal experience essay or story idea, I restricted the type of product to a children's story of 800-1,000 words directed at an elementary audience (grades three-five). The decision to restrict the scope of the personal experience essay or short story was due in part to my concern over the problem of developing an adequate criteria sheet for evaluation of the product, guiding students in writing to a potentially unfamiliar audience, and having time to emphasize the qualities of salable children's literature.

In gathering ideas for the product, my classes relied on my favorite experts in the field of children's literature—Shel Silverstein, Dr. Seuss, Judy Blume, Hans Christian Andersen, Katherine Mansfield, and Lewis Carroll. After looking at examples from these authors, the class developed a list of topics including sibling rivalry, relatives, holidays, birthdays, teachers, school situations, frightening or embarrassing times, and "subtle" persuasive techniques. In addition to this list, I supplied ideas generated from my own experiences at this age and from listening to students talk as they entered or left the classroom.

I duplicated the product scope and sequence from the curriculum guide as a starting point for various ways of presenting a personal account. We discussed such possibilities as a diary, a handbook of "techniques," a short story, an informal essay, a comic book, and an anecdote.

After collecting a sizable number of topics and presentation forms, I shared a personal experience with the students. I chose my experience as a first-grader crossing a wood and cable suspension bridge for the first time on the way to school—a school on the other side of the Snake River in St. Maries, Idaho. Of course, if you are my age (forty something), you may have to contend with such comments as, "Were there public schools way back then?" After assuring the students that, strange as it may seem, I did arrive on the planet a considerable time after Neanderthal man, and even the horse and buggy, I share my experience of trying to crawl across this bridge as it swayed in the wind and my breakfast crawled up my throat. They especially enjoy the "disgusting" breakfast part.

Armed with a criteria sheet outlining all the aspects of evaluation for the product and what I hope will answer 90 percent of their questions, the students begin exploring their pasts.

During the six-week period that this project is assigned, the students have ample time for experimentation and feedback. From the initial stages of the product, the students know that this is one of approximately six products that they must refine for display. So, there is ample motivation for them to do a good job on it.

Since the time I first used this idea, our school has established a computer lab. Had this lab been available at the time the students were writing their children's books, they could have checked the readability level of their work, assigned a reading level, incorporated computer graphics, and corrected their initial drafts easily. I strongly suggest that if you have one available, you put your school's computer lab to use—especially during the final stages of the products' development.

Over the years, I have used this idea with variations in audience and presentation. For example, one year I had the students address a freshman audience and allowed more latitude in type of presentation. As a result, some students wrote handbooks for incoming freshmen, warning them of the perils of high school; some analyzed the types of teachers found in a high school setting; others isolated certain subject areas that offer "interesting" expenditures, such as band, drivers' education, chemistry, and foreign language. Other students chose to develop such ideas as a dictionary of "types" of high school students, a manual on dating tips, anecdotes on the pitfalls of baby sitting or other part-time jobs, a "cookbook" approach to surviving adolescence, and a short history of beauty "torture devices."

The only limits that I impose on the topic selections are that they not be ones addressed by the previous years' classes and that the topics be personal but not intimate. If the criteria sheet is general in nature, it may be used again or with few modifications. By varying the audience, the topics, and the method of presentation, this idea can be used year after year without becoming repetitious or stale.

In eliciting any type of student product, I have found the following guidelines to be especially effective:

- Aim for quality not quantity. A few quality products worthy of display or publication are far more valuable to everyone involved than a closet full of mediocre ones; these are likely to remain in the closet.
- Develop a criteria sheet for evaluation of the product at the time the assignment is made. Assign weights or values to each item on the criteria sheet at this time. This effort will guide the conscientious students, but be aware that some will stuff it in their algebra book and forget they ever had it. Furthermore, the criteria sheet will facilitate the grading of the product, will prevent the pitfall of being overly impressed by only one outstanding aspect of a product, and will clearly define the type of product desired.
- Allow products to be natural out-growths of the content being studied. The personal experience product emphasizes that literature is a representation of human experiences, and nothing is as marvelous, entertaining, or strange as real life.
- Let the product of one unit of study demonstrate understanding of another unit. For example, if poetry is studied as a unit, then poetry can become a product to illustrate understanding of a novel. My sophomore classes have written ballads to illustrate their understanding of *To Kill a Mockingbird*. This approach reinforces content previously studied. Also, poetry can be used to analyze poetry. My Advanced Placement English class analyzed the structure and theme of a ballad from the Medieval period by writing a ballad on a ballad.

Works Cited

Kaplan, S.N. (1979) *Inservice training manual: activities for developing curriculum for the gifted/talented.* Ventura: Ventura County Superintendent of Schools Office.

Ward (1961). *Differential Education for the Gifted.* Columbus, Ohio: Charles E. Merrill.

Millie Goode is an English teacher in Kingsville Independent School District, Kingsville, Texas (78363).

Chapter 4

Learning Across
The Disciplines

Alluring Journeys—G/T Educational Travel
Traveling With G/T Students Promises Many Rewards, But Begin Planning Now

By Marte Clark

Educational travel is an exciting technique for involving students in their own education and for applying principles of experimental education to the G/T classroom. It is also a memorable, pleasant, and rewarding experience for the teachers, students, and families involved. Advanced preparation can help to ensure that the travel experience will be not only the ultimate in "hands on" education but also a chance to build group cohesiveness and trust.

The preparation for a major trip begins months in advance. There is no substitute for research. Have students do some reading and talk to people who have traveled to the area in which they are interested. You must have some notion of where you want to go and what you want to see and do. The more you and your students read and the more people you talk to, the more you learn about the area and the "extra-ordinary" experiences available. It is these experiences that turn a typical tourist outing into a travel adventure.

For example, are you aware that one out of every ten baseball players in the major leagues is from Latin America? Perhaps you also know that these U.S. teams support farm teams in Latin America and send players there to hone their skills. We discovered this in Merida, the capital city of the Yucatan. Street kids use paper milk cartons for gloves and play baseball whenever they are not selling roses, woven bracelets, or Chicklets to the tourists.

We arrived during the play-offs and found that we were sharing the hotel with two of the teams. Two of our student "diplomats," Jennifer and Porcia, began collecting autographs and ended up having all of our kids practically adopted by both teams. The U.S. players were thrilled to have our students to talk to, and the Hispanic players decided that their national honor was at stake if everyone did not have a good time. They proudly offered to show everyone the area's sights. Baseball was the only thing that everyone had in common, but it proved to be more than sufficient.

Though all travel agents have access to basically the same information concerning trips, some are more willing than others to search for bargains and to accommodate the special needs of your group. Inexpensive trips suitable for the students' and teacher's wallets are out there. The trick is to find them.

Begin by contacting several travel agencies. Explain what you have in mind and any budgetary constraints that you are working under. You will need to tell them the price range, so you should know your group and what they can afford. You will also need to have some minimal standards concerning your accommodations (i.e., do you require air conditioning or a bathroom in each room?). You will quickly see which travel company is willing to work with you.

Pre-packaged tours are available to just about everywhere. These are usually very well organized and tightly scheduled. The agents design the packages to appeal to tourists and to show you what the travel company thinks a tourist would like to see. If you do not like to adhere to rigid schedules or want to soak up more local culture and native ambiance, you may want to arrange your own activities once you arrive at your destination which is usually cheaper. In order to do this, you must do your homework. Allow time the first day to exchange currency and to begin arranging side trips. Have a schedule in mind but remain flexible and open to suggestion.

Schedule your most expensive and physically demanding side-trips first. Otherwise, people run out of money or lose interest in extra excursions as they begin to get tired of traveling. The end of the trip should be less hectic than the beginning. By winding down the trip with a relaxing activity, the group members will retain positive memories of an enjoyable journey. On trips lasting a week or more, you may need to allow a day for unstructured relaxation every three or four days.

Most areas have a tourist season and an "off season." By arranging your trips for the "off season," your financial savings will be substantial. Fewer tourists in the area will also mean that your group will not have as much competition for limited resources. You should also be able to experience more of the local color and fabric of the culture.

Local guides can be both interesting and fun. They can also become very tiresome. If you do not want to be guided, say so. If you start with a guide and begin to feel uncomfortable, say so. Often guides will want to show you everything there is to see in the shortest possible time. If you need to save some of the touring for another day, say so. To make your trip an exciting and rewarding experience, you must value your own instincts, skills, and knowledge.

In fact, you may want to dispense with guides altogether. That is what we did when traveling this summer to Cancun, Mexico's leading resort area. We decided that we wanted to journey to the rustic land of the Maya by day, and return to the comfort of the beach resort at night. In Cancun, we saw iguana basking on the rocks beside the sidewalks, bargained like thieves in the markets, enjoyed the world

famous folklore ballet, and were serenaded at lunch by costumed wait-
ers singing Spanish opera.

Leaving the city, we traveled down the coast to the ruins at Talum.
Since we conducted our own tour, our time was our own. We saw the
ruins at our own pace then retired to the beach to rest. Once refreshed,
we moved on to Xel-ha where we spent the rest of the day swimming
with the fish in the lagoon. The fish come there to be fed and are almost
tame. They make fascinating swimming companions. The local children delight in throwing food around the tourists which causes the fish
to swirl around you in a vivid dance of color and scales.

We had done our homework, so we knew what we wanted to see
and do. Our research enabled us to embark on our trips immediately
and to know how to arrange for transportation. We also had a good
idea of what our excursions should cost. We avoided commercial tours
and the large tourist boats and ferries. The various guidebooks that we
carried became indispensable parts of our apparel. We also talked to
the local residents and relied heavily on their advice. It does not take
long to establish who is a reliable source of information and who is not.

When members of the group went fishing, scuba diving, snorkel-
ing, or traveling to the Isla Mujeres, we hired a smaller craft to take
us. The captains and their boats were all licensed by the government,
and were able to give us more attention than the larger operations. We
bargained with taxi drivers for the cheapest possible fares and tried
the local bus system. The residents also told us where to go horseback
riding, the cheapest places to rent vehicles, how to get to Merida for
five dollars, and about the campground at Kai Luum which offers every
luxury—except electricity.

Involve group members from the beginning. Involvement must
start with data gathering and continue through decision making and
goal setting. Students involved in helping to establish the purpose of
the trip and the choice of what activities to engage in upon arrival have
a much greater sense of ownership concerning the trip. Once they
begin to share in the responsibility for making the trip a success, a possible passive experience becomes an action filled group effort.

Initially, this may be a very different role for students who are
not accustomed to being involved in the planning or research stages
of a trip. Studying cultural, archeological, and geographical elements
of the area that you are to visit is invaluable.

Breaking the research up into individual and group projects trans-
forms the trip from "your trip" to "our trip." Be certain that your topics are all relevant to what you will be seeing. Students who are accustomed to using dated references to do "encyclopedic" reports on the
amount of grain tonnage imported each year may need extra help and

structure. Guidebooks, magazines, travel sections of the newspaper, and the tourist secretariat of the country you plan to visit can provide students with timely information.

If you are going to an area where the food is going to be very different, you may want to have food as a research project. It is helpful to prepare typical foods from the region for the travelers to sample before going. The students and their families can help to identify people that have traveled to your area and to arrange for interviews or speakers for the class. Some students may want to help consult travel agents when you are beginning to collect prices.

Introduce the idea of a trip very early in the course. Regardless of whether you are attempting to go across town, to the state capitol, or on an international excursion, you need plenty of time to prepare. Your first hurdle will be to convince the students that with everyone's help, you really can accomplish the travel plan. Idle talk must quickly evolve into planning and action. Otherwise, some of the more negative students may convince the others that it is "all talk" and not worth the effort to get involved. Another hurdle may be the over exuberant. Of the twenty-five people we had sign-up to go to Mexico last year, only fourteen actually went.

Since I teach anthropology at both a high school and a junior college, I can draw students from both for the trip. We also open the trips up to the families of the travel group. I enjoy the interaction that comes from mixing ages and lifestyles. Decide in advance what size and type of group with which you are comfortable working. Also, as you begin putting the trip together, be certain that you know how many travelers you need to secure your group rate. Networking with teachers in other departments and other schools can also be helpful in putting a group together.

One of the most important aspects of the trip will be the sharing and bonding that result from the group interaction. People that remain aloof or isolate themselves from the group will miss out on a very significant part of the travel experience.

However, avoid making group members feel as though they are joined at the hip. They must not be afraid to say "no." Respect the wishes and needs of each individual. Be understanding when an individual does not want to attend a particular activity or eat in a certain restaurant. Some weary travelers may simply need some time alone to rejuvenate.

Each person brings unique talents and skills with them that will contribute greatly to the group's comfort and enjoyment. Group members must learn to respect these talents and to accommodate each person to apply that in which they excel or are comfortable.

For instance, on a recent trip to the Yucatan Peninsula, we traveled with a 70 plus year old Italian grandmother, Nana, who was multilingual. Her language facility proved to be invaluable. She gained us entry to some very notable experiences of which we would not have been aware had she not been along to chat with the locals. Because of her, some of the hotel staff threw a farewell party for us before we left.

Usually the travelers will discover hidden talents when called upon to serve the group effort. "The Skinners" (so named by one of our guides when he was trying to tell me to put the two skinny ones in the front seat) were the youngest members of our group. They also turned out to be the best shoppers and bargain hunters. They were able to save us money and make our shopping trips adventures!

Do not limit educational travel to international excursions. Every community has invaluable resources to expand the pedagogical experience. Just moving an activity off campus and involving the community lends an entirely new dimension to what the students are learning.

The interaction between student and community legitimize what the students are accomplishing. They see that the community values and supports their efforts. The involved members of the community will find the experience equally rewarding. They have the opportunity to work with bright, committed young people in an "adult" setting.

The adults are usually amazed by how beautifully the students rise to the occasion. Our classes have held legislative simulations in the community center, trials at the courthouse, Model United Nations sessions at the local university, and debates at city hall.

When government classes choose to go to the state capitol, our local legislators arrange for the students to conduct experimental simulations at times when the legislature is not in session and attend meetings when they are. Various dignitaries (including cabinet members, legislators, and the governor) have asked us to question and answer sessions. It is hard to determine who learns more from these sessions.

Want to teach about bureaucracy? Give your students your district's guidelines on field trips and ask them to arrange the trip. They will experience more bureaucracy than they ever thought possible.

Educational travel is potentially one of the most exciting and rewarding pedagogical experiences available to teachers and students alike. To ensure a safe and fascinating expedition, do your homework, trust your group, and above all—trust yourself.

Marte Clark teaches at Pinallas County High School and at Saint Petersburg Junior College (Clearwater, Florida 32625).

Another Fine Mess...
Encouraging Problem Solving Skills
With A Futuristic Dilemma

By Joel McIntosh And Bruce Doolittle

We are shut up in schools and college recitation rooms for ten or fif-teen years, and come out at last with a bellyful of words and do not know a thing.
— *Ralph Waldo Emerson*

Over one-hundred and fifty years ago, Emerson saw a weakness in education present even today. We need to move our students beyond the simple acquisition of information and help them develop thinking processes designed to produce innovative ideas, products, and solutions.

The Creative Problem Solving (CPS) process fills this need. CPS is a formal approach to developing the creative skills of students. The process allows teachers to deliberately and confidently teach students to think creatively. This article was designed to offer teachers already familiar with the CPS process an exciting activity to help their students practice problem solving skills. For teachers unfamiliar with the process, a list of resources offering a thorough coverage of the CPS Process has been provided (see "Learning to Facilitate the Process," page 94).

In *Encouraging Creative Learning for the Gifted and Talented* (1980), Don Treffinger explains that in order to prepare students to apply the process to real-world dilemmas, teachers should expose them to the techniques of CPS and allow students to apply those techniques to practice or simulated problems.

Practice problems are an exciting method for helping students master the CPS process. A practice problem (called a "mess") original-ly developed for use at Baylor University's Interdisciplinary Creative Problem Solving Conference for Secondary Gifted Students and Their Teachers is included with this article (see "Breakthrough at LongeTech," page 95-96).

In "Breakthrough," a German scientist has discovered a process which when applied to a developing human fetus, halts the aging process in the subject after the age of 25. This procedure promises both great benefits and great troubles. This is just the kind of mess which offers rich opportunity for the creative problem solver.

The CPS process is a six-step process designed to help individuals productively address the problems around them or offered to them in the case of a pre-designed mess. Isaksen and Treffinger (1985) identify these six steps.

During this step in the process, students identify a general topic area ("mess") on which to apply the rest of the process. In many CPS simulation activities such as the one presented on pages 95-96, the mess is presented to the students in the form of a classroom simulation or problem.

After presenting one of these messes to a class, time should be taken to discuss the mess with students and answer any questions related to the text of the mess. However, because messes are, by nature, "messy" or ambiguous, questions and answers at this time should be kept at a minimum.

During this step, students take an inventory of what they know, need to know, or would like to know about the selected mess. In order to find the information they need to know to address the mess, they may conduct group or independent research, group discussions, and interviews with experts.

This is an excellent point in the process to involve local experts with your gifted students. After having your students generate a list of the information they presently know about the mess and what they need to know about the mess, experts from the community may be asked to visit the class in order to answer some of the students' questions. For example, "Breakthrough at LongeTech" offers plenty of opportunity for an open discussion with experts from the fields of medicine, pharmaceuticals, politics and government, ethics and religion, and social sciences. Independent or group research may still be necessary even after "briefings" from local experts.

Early in this step, students generate as many possible problem statements as they are able. Then they narrow their choices to a single statement of a problem associated with the mess. Because the way the problem is defined so profoundly affects the solutions generated, this is a very important step in the CPS process.

All generated problems should begin with the stems "In what ways might we ..." or "How might we ..." For example in "Breakthrough at LongeTech," students might generate such problems as "In what ways might we regulate the distribution of this new medical process," "How might we reduce the impact of this new process on the world's population size," and "In what ways might we provide adequate housing and sustenance for the larger population resulting from this new process."

Early in this step, students identify many possible ways of addressing the identified problem. By this step's conclusion, the students will have narrowed their generated list of possible solutions to only a few very strong possibilities.

In "Breakthrough at LongeTech," students might generate ideas for solving the dilemma with innovative housing programs, increased international regulation of drug-testing, nationalization of the medical industry, etc.

During this step, students identify a set of criteria to evaluate the many ideas they generated for solving their problem. They then evaluate their solutions and identify a single solution for their problem. At this time, students often use an evaluation grid or some other evaluation tool in order to choose the best solution to their problem.

The generated criteria in "Breakthrough" might include, "To what extent will the solution maintain present living conditions," "To what extent will the technology required to implement the solution be available," or "To what extent is this solution likely to receive the support of this country's population." The students then use their selected list of criteria to choose their strongest solution.

During this step, students generate a plan of action designed to implement their solution. A plan of action should include ways of overcoming obstacles to the implementation of a plan and ways of effectively using those who would assist in the implementation of the solution.

For example, a plan of action designed to restrict the application of the medical procedure in "Breakthrough" would have to offer methods for overcoming the black market which such a restriction might spawn. "Assisters" for the solution might include potential investors in the process, various governmental agencies, or even environmental groups concerned about the process' impact on the environment.

Keep in mind that it is not always necessary to go through every one of the steps in the CPS process. For example, in "Breakthrough," students move into the CPS process after being presented the mess. In other situations, students might be presented with a pre-designed problem statement, or they might be asked to select from a list of predefined solutions.

One of the strengths of the CPS process is this flexibility. As a teacher becomes more familiar with the process, not only will the idea of moving in and out of the process at different points become comfortable, but the idea of mixing simulations, role-playing, socio-drama, lectures, and independent research with the various steps of the CPS process will seem quite natural as well.

The mess on pages 95-96 was designed in such a way that a teacher need not be an "expert" in CPS facilitation in order to use the activity. However, it will be helpful if both the teacher and the students involved in this activity understand and have practiced the techniques of brainstorming and deferred judgement, have an understanding of the use of criteria for evaluation, and have an understanding of the various CPS steps and techniques.

Learning To Facilitate The Process

The following is a list of resources designed specifically for the purpose of training individuals to facilitate the CPS process.

- Baylor University's Interdisciplinary Problem Solving Conference (Waco, TX). This conference, held each March, offers secondary teachers and students training in CPS as well as interdisciplinary curriculum. Teachers receive direct instruction and observe as master teachers facilitate over one hundred gifted students applying the process to a simulated mess. More information may be obtained by writing Joel McIntosh, Baylor University, P.O. Box 97134, Waco, TX 76798-7314.
- The Center for Creative Learning (Sarasota, FL) offers one and two week Creative Problem Solving seminars for educational professionals. These programs offer intensive, small group training in the process. For more information, contact the Center at 4152 Independence Ct., Suite C-7, Sarasota, FL 34234.
- Elwell, P.A. (1990). *Creative Problem Solving for Teens*. East Aurora: D.O.K. Publishers. An excellent source of classroom activities designed to teach teachers and students the various CPS techniques.
- Treffinger, D.J. and S.G. Isaksen. (1985). *Creative Problem Solving: The Basic Course*. Buffalo: Bearly Limited. This book offers a thorough grounding in the process. It is a *must* for anyone interested in CPS.

Works Cited

Treffinger, D.J. (1980). Encouraging creative learning for the gifted and talented: a handbook of methods and techniques. Ventura: Ventura County Superintendent of Schools Office.

Treffinger, D.J. and S.G. Isaksen. (1985). Creative problem solving: the basic course. Buffalo: Bearly Limited.

Joel McIntosh is presently the editor of The Prufrock Journal. *He is also the coordinator of Baylor University's Interdisciplinary Creative Problem Solving Conference.*

Breakthrough At LongeTech
A CPS Practice Mess
Developed For Baylor University's
Interdisciplinary Creative Problem Solving Conference

In the spring of 1990, Clause Grueben, an East German genetic engineer, left his homeland along with thousands of other East Germans who took advantage of their country's new liberal border restrictions.

By April 13, 1992, Grueben had made contact with researchers at the Sorbonne in Paris. With their encouragement, Grueben called a press conference at which he made a startling claim. Stating that the aging process was due to genetic timing mechanisms, Grueben asserted that for ten years he had been developing a technique for "turning–off" the genes that cause the aging process. Grueben then shocked the scientific world by claiming that he had successfully identified a major "on/off switch" and developed a technique to turn it off. The technique, Grueben said, must be performed in vitro on a zygote which is then implanted in a host parent.

The scientist went on to say that he had actually performed the technique on thousands of laboratory rats and found it increased their life span by 3.6 times the norm.

Grueben called this result the Methuselah Effect. The scientist then claimed to have produced four viable swine (an animal whose blood closely resembles that of humans) with the process. Yet, as the life span of these animals is 25 years, Grueben could not yet speculate on any increased longevity resulting from the swine experiments.

At the time, Grueben's press conference created global interest in the scientist. As researchers closely associated with Grueben in East Germany reached the West, reporters uncovered more news of the scientist's experiments— news which tainted the scientist's claims. These researchers claimed that the process had potential side effects. Apparently, 5% of Grueben's rat subjects showed signs of severe mental aggravation which manifested itself, in extreme cases, as cannibalism and self mutilation. In another 5% of the subjects, a mysterious immune system failure developed which inevitably resulted in the animal's death. Because this latter side effect could manifest itself late in the animal's life span, it was often passed from one generation to the next. Researchers also stated that their studies made it clear that the Methuselah Effect was a recessive genetic trait. This obviously made the treatment less useful for the direct offspring of "mixed" matings. Grueben refused either to verify or deny these assertions.

In May of 1992, a California genetic research facility called LongeTech, a company founded in the mid–1980s for the purpose of furthering research into human longevity, hired Grueben. The scientist and LongeTech successfully engineered a media blackout concerning his work at the company, and media attention eventually moved on to other concerns.

The public heard little of Grueben until December 3, 1994. On that day Grueben called a press conference to make an astounding claim. According to Grueben, he and LongeTech had genetically altered the aging genes in a human zygote which, after implantation in a host human, had developed into a healthy baby. To verify the process, Grueben produced research data generated at Cal Tech on the baby. The data indicated that the baby's genetic make–up had been altered. Grueben also produced a number of Cal Tech scientists who had successfully created the Methuselah Effect in laboratory rats. These scientists could not, however, discuss their work as LongeTech had applied for a patent on the process whose secret was now legally protected.

Officials at LongeTech stated at the press conference that Grueben's process would be available commercially before the end of 1995. They went on to say the technique would cost as much as $100,000 but could cost as little as $10,000 within 10 to 15 years.

Days after the press conference, the president created the Committee on Human Longevity—a body composed of representatives from many governmental departments and private organizations. The president charged the committee with the task of identifying the significant problem associated with LongeTech's new technique and to offer the most promising solution to that problem.

College Databank
An Independent Project For College Bound Students

By Thomas Sipe

I face many challenges as Coordinator of Gifted Education at a large, suburban high school. Stimulating productive independent study is certainly among them. Fortunately, the microcomputer has given me a new and highly effective tool to meet this challenge as it is well-suited to the individualization that is paramount to gifted education. Since the development of communication skills and critical thinking skills is important for many of my students, I designed the College Databank as an independent study tool to address those basic needs and encourage the exploration of the computer as a productivity tool.

Grade Level
Senior High

Objectives
- Develop critical thinking skills
- Develop communication skills
- Develop word processing skills
- Develop database management skills

Student interest in both colleges and computers provides the motivation that drives this long-term project. The benefits are three-fold. First, students practice the critical thinking skills of comparison and contrast as well as evaluation. Second, the purposeful use of the computer promotes an appreciation of the computer as a tool and encourages further exploration of its potential. And third, the project forces students to communicate effectively.

While it is not difficult to glean a general description, a list of majors, and certain statistics about a college or university from a number of prepared sources, it is difficult to find more significant, unbiased, or personal information.

Providing just such a source was the purpose behind our College Databank project. The database at the core of this project is student produced and managed. It relies on objective data gathered in the usual ways and on subjective data gathered from recent graduates. Focusing on those schools being attended by high school graduates from our community, this database has immediate value to the students who produce it and other students simply using it.

Materials

- Works integrated software (AppleWorks, GreatWorks, or Microsoft Works)
- Any standard college guide
- College catalogs
- Computer and printer

Procedures

Phase 1

- Since the integrated software will be the primary tool used for this project, students are first given a brief introduction to the software by the instructor and then allowed to work independently through the tutorials provided with the software. The instructor should be on hand to answer questions as needed.
- Provided with data from the Guidance Office, students will then create the first of several related Works databases. This will be a simple file that will identify graduates who are attending post-secondary schools, the names of their schools, and their addresses.
- Through brainstorming the students will produce a list of topics that will become the basis for a survey to be mailed to the college students.
- Using the Works word processor, they will develop a form letter and survey that will be sent to the college students.
- Again using the word processor, the students will produce form letters merged with names and addresses from the database. (For many, this will be their first experience with merging data into a form. It is rewarding to see their recognition of the power this gives the computer user.) The student should also produce the appropriate mailing labels at this time.
- Immediately after mailing the surveys, the students should create a "thank you" letter to be sent as the responses come in. As before, the students may create a form letter for this purpose.

Note: At this point in the project, students will be enthusiastic about computer use, but the instructor should stress basic communication skills such as clarity and courtesy. It is also imperative that this phase is completed quickly and efficiently to allow time for the response cycle.

Phase 2

- Using the list of schools generated in Phase 1, students should begin creating the Databank by creating two files for each college. The first file should be in traditional database format and should include such things as name and address of the school, phone number of the admissions office, SAT and grade point requirements, a brief description of the school's academic offerings, distance from the home community, size, housing, comments, and names of graduates who attended the school. Students gather all this information from college catalogs or commercial guides. Additionally, there should be a field that would hold the guide word used to name the subjective file described below.
- Students should start the subjective Databank by creating a word processor file for each school in the database. The guide word will serve as the file name for these files. Each file should be headed with the full name and address of the school and a brief paragraph of description.
- As responses to the letters in Phase 1 arrive, the students should enter the remarks in the appropriate file. For example, when a student at Pitt remarks, "I wish I had taken more math in high school," this remark is appended to the file for the University of Pittsburgh noting the student's name and major if possible.
- The spreadsheet component of the integrated software is brought into play at this point. The students should create a spreadsheet to hold financial data about the schools. The students create columns for tuition, housing, miscellaneous expenses, etc. Totals per school and averages are then easily calculated. (Once students discover graphing capabilities here, they will want to create any of number of graphs to synthesize the information in the spreadsheet.)
- Once the Databank is completed the instructor may want to employ students as peer tutors. (They will be eager to see the data they have collected and organized be used and will want to teach their friends how to search the Databank as well as how to print the relevant files.)

Phase 3

Upon completion of the Databank, the students should write an essay that identifies the college they would select from those listed and enumerates the reasons. If needed, the instructor should review the strategies of successful comparison and contrast and offer any other writing instruction necessary.

Summary

Because of their power and ease of use, Microsoft Works or GreatWorks provide the perfect vehicles for this project. Through the use of windows, students are able to call up both the objective and subjective databases simultaneously. The word processor encourages students to edit their work, creating the database forms is visually logical and easily accomplished, and the merge and graphing functions drive home the real power of computing. AppleWorks offers many, but not all, of the same advantages.

The Databank itself is useful to the students who produce it and others who are beginning the college search. What is more important, however, is the fact that the project has encouraged the students to use critical thinking and to develop communication skills while seeing the microcomputer as an invaluable tool.

Sample Subjective File

Carnegie-Mellon University

Highly respected, CMU is considered one of the top engineering schools in the country and is also nationally known for its fine arts department. Additionally, CMU offers an extensive list of majors and individually designed curricula. It is a city campus located in Oakland and adjoins the University of Pittsburgh. The museums of natural history and art and an extensive library at nearby Carnegie Institute offer students many opportunities for research and study.

Student Remarks:

"Mr. Bernard's Advanced Chemistry was good preparation for my first chemistry classes here."
Linda Williams, Chemical Engineering

"What I used to like best is that it is close and I can come home on weekends, but now what I like is that there is so much to do in the city!"
Adam Thomas, American Studies

"We do a lot of work with the city developing the Technology Park down by the river, and that's fun."
Jim Randall, Computer Science

Sample Objective File

Carnegie-Mellon University

Guide Word: CMU
Updated: 10/90
Size: 7000
Miles from Irwin: 30
Description: Four-year, coed, comprehensive, very selective
Housing: On and off campus, Coed housing available
Comprehensive Cost: $17,400
SAT: Verbal, 78%; Math, 94%
Address: Pittsburgh, PA 15213
Phone: (412) 268-2082
Student Contacts: Linda Williams, Adam Thomas, Bob Jergens, Chris Lynn, Jim Randall

Software References

AppleWorks
For Apple II Series Computers
Claris Software
P.O. Box 526
Santa Clara, CA 95052

GreatWorks
For Macintosh Computers
Symantec
10201 Torre Avenue
Cupertino, CA 95014

Microsoft Works
For Macintosh or IBM compatible Computers
MicroSoft Software
One Microsoft Way
Redmond, WA 98052

Thomas Sipe is the presently coordinator of Gifted Education for Norwin Senior High School, North Huntingdon, PA 15642.

Creative Problem Solving
The Need, The Process, The Metamorphosis

By Dr. Don J. Treffinger & Marion R. Sortore

Adolescents in today's society are often expected to think and behave as adults. In fact, educators, parents and adolescents themselves prefer to use the descriptions, "young men and women" or "young adults," rather than "teen" or "adolescent." These young adults go to school, but they also dress, socialize, and hold jobs as part of the adult world. However, increased stresses and pressures also come hand in hand with adult activities.

Young men and women today are pressured at an early age (as early as 7th grade) to make choices that may have far-reaching impact on their adult lives. Their search for identity (status, vocational and sexual) is made more difficult by the many complex issues facing them: moral development; values (personal, political, and religious); relationships with peers; love and sex; drugs; family situations; careers; and school. Young adults learn in high schools today what many of their parents did not encounter until they were in college. They face decisions and problems that are increasingly complex and difficult as they grow up in a world of rapid social and technological change.

With this increased exposure to all aspects of an adult life, young adults need constructive models, provided by adults who themselves know and apply a variety of methods and strategies to be productive and effective. Raven (1984, pp. 187-200), as an outgrowth of a series of studies in Ireland and in Britain, compiled an extensive review of competencies exhibited by successful adults, which he described as components of competence. These refer to the characteristics and abilities which enable people to reach their valued goals. Among the competencies described by Raven are those listed in Table One. Similar characteristics have been described by Torrance (1979), MacKinnon (1978), Amabile (1983), and others who have explored the characteristics associated with creativity

Where will students in school today find the processes they need to deal effectively and productively with the challenges of adulthood? Do we expect students to learn these skills on their own, when they tackle their first big "real world" problem? Will they become adults who deal with problems and challenges by "trial and error," using only whatever strategies they might learn by chance or accident?

We believe that it is possible—and important—to offer young adults opportunities to learn and apply a number of strategies or powerful "tools for the mind" that will serve them well in dealing with many of the opportunities and challenges of the adult world. If we do want students to have such tools available and "ready for use" in a wide range of situations, we should not leave them to chance. Instruction in productive thinking, problem solving, and decision-making can thus be viewed as an important aspect of learning "real life" skills for survival and success.

Table 1—Components Of Competence

- Tendency to seek and utilize feedback
- Self confidence
- Adaptability: absence of feelings of trained incapacity (Do people feel that they can master new tasks in order to achieve their goals, or do they feel that each new task requires extensive training and skills which they are not able to acquire?)
- Willingness to think ahead: tolerance for abstract thought
- Willingness to think for oneself, to be original
- Critical thinking (Are people prepared to give uncritical acceptance to what others say, to their advice, to rumor and to authority? Or do they question these things, and make deductions from such advice as can be validated or invalidated from their own experience?)
- Tolerance of cognitive complexity (To understand the complex factors which usually determine things which happen in society, to examine the issues thoroughly.)
- Willingness to work at something which is disturbing and challenging (This may be contrasted with a preference for work which is comfortable and trivial.)
- Ability to research the environment for opportunities and resources (physical and human) help, know-how, materials, insights and ideas to help achieve one's goals.
- Win-win (not "win-lose") attitudes and breadth of perspective
- Persistence
- The ability to make good decisions
- Willingness to take personal responsibility
- Ability to work with others to achieve a goal
- Ability to get others to work together effectively to achieve the goal
- Ability to listen to others and to take what they say into account
- Ability to handle conflict and differences of opinion

Involving many of the competencies described by Raven, incorporating Creative Problem Solving (CPS; Isaksen & Treffinger, 1985) into your instructional program will create opportunities to allow and help young adults draw on and use their knowledge and skills from many academic classes and life backgrounds more effectively as they become involved in "real life" problems.

Sternberg (1985, pp. 194-198) suggested that many "packaged" critical thinking programs neglect the real challenges and experiences of the everyday world, and hence ill prepare students for adult problem solving; he observed: "I have grown increasingly disturbed by the lack of correspondence between what is required for critical thinking in adulthood and what is being taught in school programs intended to develop critical thinking. We are preparing students to deal with problems that are in many respects unlike those that they will face as adults. (1985, p. 194). Sternberg described ten major differences between real problems and the activities typically presented in many "thinking skills" instructional programs:

1. In the every day world, the first and sometimes most difficult step in problem solving is the recognition that a problem exists.
2. In every day problem solving it is often harder to figure out just what the problem is than to figure out how to solve it. Having recognized the existence of a problem, it is often quite difficult to specify just what the problem is.
3. Every day problems tend to be ill-structured ... few of life's problems are so neatly structured, and it is the solving of ill-structured rather than well structured problems that will prepare us for the challenges we most often face.
4. In every day problem solving it is not usually clear just what information will be needed to solve a given problem, nor is it always clear where the requisite information can be found.
5. The solutions to everyday problems depend on and interact with the contexts in which the problems are presented ... real-world problems are deeply embedded in multiple contexts that can affect their solutions.
6. Every day problems generally have no one right solution, and even the criteria for what constitutes a best solution are often not clear.
7. The solutions of every day problems depend at least as much on informal knowledge as formal knowledge.
8. Solutions to important every day problems have consequences that matter ... solutions cannot be separated from consequences, because the solution usually depends to some extent on the possible consequences of alternative solutions.

9. Every day problem solving often occurs in groups. The same individuals who have demonstrated beyond a doubt their skill in solving problems individually seem to be at an utter loss when they approach a problem in a group.
10. Every day problems can be complicated, messy, and stubbornly persistent. (1985, pp. 194-198).

Creative Problem Solving provides a structured, systematic approach for guiding students in their efforts to deal with real problems. We emphasize that "real" problems must satisfy three fundamental criteria:

1. students must have ownership, by which we mean the opportunity to take action and carry out the solution, and the intent and responsibility to do so;
2. the problem must represent a matter of personal concern and consequence, with impact on their lives and the world around them; and
3. the students want and need new ideas.

Using these criteria, many problems that we often describe as "real" might actually be described better or more accurately as "realistic." If the problem is drawn from the actual world of people and events in which we live, rather than simply dealing with fantasy or imaginary circumstances, we might be tempted to call it "real," such as "world hunger," "global warming," or "over-population."

Without a strong personal commitment, a search for new ideas, and, most importantly, a commitment to action, however, they fall short of our definition, and would be described as "realistic." Realistic problems can be very useful, of course, as case studies or practice problems, for instructional purposes; they are not sufficient, however, for us to conclude that we have dealt adequately with the students' needs to address and solve the kinds of problems that are encountered by adults in everyday life. What are examples of some of the real problems confronted by young adults today? Consider these possible examples, which were identified by a group of teachers in a brainstorming session on "applications of CPS within a school setting":

• Personal concerns of individuals or groups
• Comprehensive School Improvement planning
• Program planning or curriculum design
• School groups (e.g., student council, Yearbook, etc.)
• School issues, concerns, special events

- School policies (*e.g.,* discipline, privileges, dress, etc.)
- Classroom management policies and procedures
- Fund-raising
- Independent Study Projects, Individual or Small Group Investigations of Problems in various content areas
- Planning special projects for contests or competitions (*e.g.,* Science Fair, Talent Show, other programs)
- Working with "clients" within the school (students, teachers, other staff, parent groups)
- Working with outside clients—enhance cooperation and mutual involvement of School/Community

When we conducted a similar brainstorming session (on "ways of using CPS") with secondary school students, however, a much more extensive list of opportunities and concerns emerged. The students' list is presented in Table Two.

Unfortunately, some students, and many adults, have grown up with the belief that a "problem" is a negative situation—something wrong, something troublesome, annoying, frustrating, or needing to be repaired—to be dealt with as quickly as possible, or perhaps even hidden and ignored until it goes away. In CPS, we encourage people to take a fresh look at "problems" by thinking of them as opportunities, challenges, or invitations to generate and use some promising new ideas. Through a constructive, affirmative approach to finding, defining, and solving "problems," CPS responds to the special challenges that young adults face by providing them with tools and strategies that make people more powerful, giving them positive options, and helping them to be confident and competent in facing real life problems. In a young adult's search for identity the CPS process offers a constructive path for exploring new situations, generating ideas for handling those situations, and making action plans to carry out their solutions successfully.

Two fundamental principles (Deferred Judgment and Affirmative Judgment) are the basic foundation for the Creative Problem Solving process. Deferred judgment reminds problem solvers that praise and criticism of ideas can stifle the "flow" or generation of ideas, so the process of generating ideas should be separated from the task of analyzing or evaluating them. When we do turn our attention to analysis and evaluation, the principle of Affirmative Judgment reminds us to examine ideas carefully and thoroughly, but constructively; "critical" is not the same as "criticize." Thus, in evaluating options, an affirmative approach emphasizes balanced consideration of the advantages, limitations, and potentials of ideas.

Table 2—Concerns Of Secondary Students

•Cafeteria Food	•Student Council
•Homework	•School Fund Raising
•Drugs	•Long Term Projects
•Peer Pressures	•Future Careers/Decisions
•Sports	•Allowance, job, money
•Having to take lessons	•Seeming to be "different"
•Braces	•Dances
•Being introverted	•Physical, Sexual Abuse
•Independence	•Isolation
•Buying presents	•Pregnancy
•Alcohol	•Acne
•Suicide	•Threat of Nuclear War
•Moods, Emotions	•Abortion
•Transportation	•Parties
•Uncertain World Future	•Death, Aging Relatives
•B.O.	•Racism
•Pets	•Boredom
•Hobbies	•Heterosexual Relationships
•Crime, safety	•Homosexuality
•Illness, disease, AIDS	•Dealing with teachers
•Dating	•Divorce, re-marriage
•Dealing with Parents	•Cars
•Dealing with Peers, Siblings	•Extra-curricular activities
•Moving	•Making new friends
•Clothes, Fashion, Styles	•Public Speaking
•Improving Grades	•Older/Younger Brother/Sister
•Making choices	•Curfew, Staying Out
•Broken bicycle	•Watching TV, MTV
•Entering contests	•School Trip, activities
•Getting up in the morning	•Yearbook
•Choosing own clothes	•Doing our own Newspaper
•Dress Code	•Discipline, Detention, etc.
•School Rules	•Being Grounded

As these principles are applied, problem solvers begin to work deliberately and systematically on their challenge, selecting and using a variety of strategies or techniques to help them "move forward" towards a solution and an action plan. The structure of the CPS model is dynamic, and has continued to expand and be refined throughout its history of more than three decades of research, development, and implementation. In our current work, the CPS structure involves three major "components," based on the three primary tasks involved in solving a problem: understanding the problem and getting it ready to work on (which includes identifying a general challenge or goal, examining the "Mess" in many ways to determine the "key" data, and formulating a specific problem statement); generating ideas; and planning for action (which involves using criteria to choose, develop, and refine promising solutions as well as planning for acceptance and implementation). These three components, encompass six stages—mess-finding, data-finding, problem-finding, idea-finding,solution-finding, and acceptance-finding. In each stage, creative problem solvers use both their divergent or creative thinking (to generate ideas or alternatives) and their convergent or critical thinking (to analyze, select, and improve promising possibilities).

In organizing instruction in CPS, we have found it helpful to describe three general levels of an effective program: providing instruction in the basic tools for creative and critical thinking, learning and practicing the CPS model, and dealing with real problems and challenges.

The first level involves providing students with the fundamental skills or strategies they will need to be able think creatively and critically. Some of these help students to generate many, varied, or unusual ideas (which we refer to as teaching the "divergent tools"); these techniques include, for example: brainstorming, what if/just suppose, attribute listing, SCAMPER, and forced relationships. Other Level One tools involve strategies for analyzing, refining, or choosing ideas (or "convergent tools"); some examples include: using analogies, comparing and contrasting, sequencing, making inferences, creating categories or "clustering" ideas, judging relevant data, and using specific techniques for comparing or selecting ideas (such as an evaluation grid or matrix). A number of these tools are summarized in Table Three.

The Level One tools are also described and illustrated in a wide variety of supplementary or "enrichment" publications, as well as in many published "thinking skills programs." [Such materials are available from many sources, of course. One catalog containing many Level One resources, from a variety of publishers, can be obtained from the Center for Creative Learning]. Level One techniques are easily integrated with classroom content, and can readily be used to support and extend students' learning in all subject areas. At the Center for Creative Learning, we have just begun an extensive new "CPS Curriculum Development Project," in which we are creating materials illustrating applications of many of the Level One Tools as well as the total CPS Process in a variety of content areas and across grade levels. During the 1990-91 school year, prototypes of these materials are undergoing field-testing in more than 25 school districts in the United

States and Canada, and we expect that they will be available for use in other schools in mid-1991. We invite inquiries from readers who are interested in learning more about these new resources.

The Level One tools are often introduced and practiced independently or directly, and then applied to content. For example: brainstorming can be taught in Earth Science. The teacher, or one or more volunteer students, serves as a recorder, writing the ideas generated by the class on the board. A general, open-ended question is presented, such as "List as many things as you can think of that you might encounter if you began digging a hole in the ground in your yard." The students might generate quite a list (dirt, worms, buried treasure, pieces of glass, rocks, etc.) The class might next categorize the items from their list, and might also use content from their Earth Science class to create or discuss their categories and the specific objects.

Table 3—Level One "Toolbox"

Divergent Tools For Generating Ideas

Brainstorming: For any open-ended question, list many possible responses. Don't praise or criticize any ideas.

What If/Just Suppose: Using imaginary examples; (e.g., "What if you had a magic wand?") or posing questions contrary to fact ("What if pigs had wings")

Attribute Listing: List the attributes of an item or situation and generate new ideas from each of the attributes.

Idea Checklists: Use words to "trigger" new ideas. Example: SCAMPER — are there ways to Substitute, Combine, Adapt, Minify/Magnify, Put to other uses, Eliminate, Reverse, or rearrange idea you generated in order to create new ideas?

Forced Relationships: Consider a word or object that seems unrelated to the problem and try to "force fit" ideas or connections from it.

Morphological Analysis: Generate many options for each of several main issues, then "mix and match" new connection.

In a creative writing class, the teacher might ask groups of four students to brainstorm as many ways as possible that an author might express a particular feeling or emotion in a character, such as fear or anger. Each group might then be asked to create a setting and a character, and to draw ideas from their list to present a particular emotion to the class in a novel or unusual way, challenging students in the other groups to identify and describe the emotion and its expression as each group presents its idea. This could easily be extended into identifying examples from literature or comparing methods employed by various authors.

A set of basic "tool" strategies, along with a rich knowledge base, provides an important part of the foundation for productive thinking and effective problem solving, but is not sufficient. Young adults also need to learn to incorporate the Level One tools and techniques into the more extensive framework of the CPS model, so the tools will be useful in solving problems and making better decisions. In Level Two, we seek to build students' competence in applying their thinking tools to problem solving as well as their confidence in their own ability to be productive thinkers. Since our goal involves "command" of the CPS process, we want to use problems that are engaging or motivational for the students, but we also want to insure that students are not so deeply invested in the content of the problem that they lose sight of the process they're learning.

Thus, Level Two represents an appropriate time for "realistic" problems, in which instructional activities involve contrived (or "canned") practice problems drawn from content areas, case studies or simulations, current events, or from any number of published practice problems (e.g., Future Problem Solving scenarios, Odyssey of the Mind problem collections, or the Practice Problems Notebook provided by the Center for Creative Learning). Elwell's (1990) book, *Creative Problem Solving for Teens,* provides a number of useful activities and exercises using familiar challenges for today's teens to offer practice in applying the six CPS stages. These challenging situations include, for example, computer dating, college search, and family friction.

At Level Two, students are also introduced to and practice the roles of *client* (the person who owns the problem on which the group is working), *facilitator* (managing the CPS process with the group), and *resource group* (people who serve as a "think tank" to help generate and analyze ideas). Finally, Level Two also involves helping students learn and use effectively the vocabulary and language of CPS, and builds other metacognitive or "executive" skills that enable students to select and apply certain tools or strategies deliberately and to recognize when particular tools might be especially useful.

When we reach Level Three, young adults become involved using CPS to deal with real problems and challenges representing their own personal or group goals, opportunities or concerns, school challenges, or community issues for which the students are concerned and committed to action. We believe that experience at Level Three is an essential component of a comprehensive CPS program, since we take seriously Sternberg's observation that, if we expect our students to deal effectively with the kind of problems and challenges the world really presents, we must offer them experience and guidance in working on them, rather than shying away or saying, "you'll be able to do that later."

Level Three does involve an important "metamorphosis," however. Students involved in using CPS with real problems, for which there will be real actions and consequences, are no longer "learning about" productive thinking and problem solving—they are practitioners of those methods. Teachers who engage students in real problem and challenges are also changing, moving beyond "covering content" and becoming involved in what might be described as "curriculum stretching." There are, of course, many pressures of time and required curricula that can increase the difficulty of dealing with Level Three in a school setting. We believe, however, that if we are serious about curriculum reform, challenging our students at higher levels and in new ways, and preparing students to become effective participants in a new and changing world, it is imperative that we create and carry out opportunities for work at Level Three.

Many school districts are actively using the CPS model and the success stories are as varied as the schools. For example: in the Honeoye Central School System in Honeoye, New York, the cafeteria manager had a particularly messy situation. It was the intention of the cafeteria to keep costs down and at the same time be environmentally conscious. To meet these goal the cafeteria decided to use dishes as opposed to styrofoam. They were appalled when students began throwing the dishes away instead of returning them. In one day the cafeteria lost 93 out of 100 soup bowls! The cafeteria manager became a client for a CPS session, and presented this messy situation to a resource group of Honeoye Students. The students, facilitator and client worked together in a series of five, forty-five minute sessions. At the conclusion the cafeteria manager had in her possession an action plan that included a campaign to enlighten students and parents to the problem, and a design for a garbage can cover which would allow only paper products to be thrown away. The students themselves drew posters and wrote newsletter articles and waged an impressive campaign. The cafeteria manager enlisted the help of the custodial staff who built the cover for the garbage can. So effective was the implementation of the action plan that in a two month period only one dish was missing. (The cafeteria manager thanked the resource group with free ice cream sundaes.)

In the same school system another "Mess" provided an excellent opportunity for CPS in action. The parking lot was a disaster waiting to happen. There was no system for busses to discharge students and for parents to discharge students. With the Transportation Director and Superintendent of schools as clients, Honeoye students tackled the problem. The result was a new blueprint and written plan for completely redesigning the parking area. These plans were presented to the School Board and approved. Contractors were hired and the new parking lot and plan are in place today.

CPS has also been implemented at Level Three in a number of other secondary schools with whose teachers we have worked in recent years. For example, at the Lakewood, Ohio, High School, many students have also used CPS to work with individuals and organizations from their community to solve real problems, and one teacher's duties include specific responsibilities as a "Community Client Coordinator," seeking people to provide new problems for eager problem solvers to tackle. Across the continent, from east (e.g., Newark, New York,) to west (e.g., Duncan, British Columbia), students at both the elementary and secondary levels have worked on real problems in their school and community, and have been instrumental in creating successful solutions that have been carried into action.

Although CPS is not a panacea for the troubles and challenges of young adults today, it gives them a constructive set of tools to use in their lives to work through the challenges they face. With mastery of the CPS Process students will attain control of the outcome of problems; they will discover and develop possible solutions to real life problems, and construct a plan of action that allows them to control the implementation of the solution. A word of caution is in order, however: Once young adults have completed the metamorphosis from absorbers of knowledge to problem solvers, or from "learners" to dynamic, involved concerned citizens, and once they have been "empowered" to meet real life challenges, they will not accept too meekly returning to the cocoon.

Students who have been actively involved in CPS, and who see the results in action, will continue to search for and be involved in productive thinking and problem solving, and they will press us to establish and maintain high levels of challenge through the school program.

Works Cited

Amabile, T. M. (1983). *The social psychology of creativity.* New York: Springer Verlag.

Elwell, P. A. (1990). *Creative problem solving for teens.* East Aurora, NY: DOK.

Isaksen, S. G. & Treffinger, D. J. (1985). *Creative problem solving: the basic course.* Buffalo, NY: Bearly Limited.

MacKinnon, D. W. (1978). *In search of human effectiveness.* Buffalo, NY: Bearly Limited.

Raven, J. (1984). *Competence in modern society.* London: H. K. Lewis and Company.

Sternberg, R. J. (1985). Teaching critical thinking: are we making critical mistakes? Part I. *Phi Delta Kappan, 67 (3),* 194-198.

Torrance, E. P. (1979). *The search for Satori and creativity.* Buffalo, NY: Bearly Limited.

Don Treffinger is the director of the Center for Creative Learning, Professor of Creative Studies at the State University College at Buffalo, and author of numerous texts about CPS and gifted education. Marion Sortore is the director of gifted education at Honeoye School and an adjunct staff member at the Center for Creative Learning.

For The Common Good
Teaching Idea Generation And Evaluation
With A Futuristic Simulation

By Joel McIntosh

I designed this lesson to give teachers of almost any discipline a high-ly motivational way to teach productive thinking skills. During the lesson students generate creative ideas and learn to evaluate those ideas using a process of selecting and applying criteria. The lesson has the added benefit of making students more aware of the ethical, scientific, and governmental challenges offered by the growing scientific field of bio-engineering.

In this unit, students —

- Generate ideas using a set of guidelines for divergent thought
- Apply a systematic evaluation process in order to make a decision
- Identify potential problems caused by the extension of the human life span
- Project trends in bio-engineering into the future
- Articulate a value or ethical position related to bio-engineering

For the Common Good includes two parts. The first is a direct-teach activity in which students learn the basics of idea generation and evaluation. In the second, the students apply the process to a simulated situation.

If your students are familiar with the process of selecting and applying criteria for evaluation, you may skip the next section and read the section titled "The Simulation." If, however, your students are new to the process, it will be necessary to teach it using the lesson below.

Direct-Teach

Preparation
- Make one copy of the evaluation grid for each student (page 125)
- Make an overhead of the evaluation grid (optional)

The Lesson

Start the lesson by asking if any of your students play a sport, play a musical instrument, or participate in any activity which requires great skill and concentration. After taking a sampling of the various things your students are interested in, ask those who play golf or tennis what happens when they begin thinking about what they are doing as they play the sport. That is, what happens to tennis players when they begin thinking about their grip, stance, or backhand while playing an intense game. The students' answers will vary, but the gist will be that the players' game is hindered.

Then discuss with your students how taking lessons from an expert effects their game. Ask them if they have ever taken lessons from a coach or professional. Ask if the expert's suggestions improved their play immediately or if the suggestions actually made play more difficult at first. Generally, students will explain that it made play more difficult. In fact, some may explain that they were so frustrated with their new level of play that they disregarded the expert's advice and went back to their own style.

Next, explain that thinking is like playing a sport. Most of the time, we go through life without really thinking about how we think. Like any good athlete or musician, we play our thinking game most efficiently by just doing it. If we constantly had to think about the process we use to make decisions, we would be very poor thinkers indeed!

Then explain that like good athletes who ask an expert to help fine tune their game, we sometimes need to fine-tune the process we use to make decisions. Explain that you are about to show them one model for the way we make decisions by playing a game in which they create the "perfect" Saturday night.

Tell them that there are only five rules for the first part of the game.

* Don't make judgments about anyone's ideas
* Come up with lots of ideas
* Accept "way-out" or "off-the-wall" ideas
* "Stretch" your thinking even when you are all out of ideas
* Join or combine any ideas you like

Ask students to brainstorm the various things they might do on a Saturday night. As students call out their Saturday night activities, write them on the board. After the students have generated a few ideas, help them generate more by prompting them with the following questions:

- Where might you go instead of going to the _____ (mention one of the ideas already listed)?
- What could you do along with doing _____ (mention one of the ideas already listed)?
- If you added something to _____ (mention one of the ideas already listed) what would you add?
- If you only had an hour and a half, what might you do?
- What is a completely different or new way of doing _____ (mention one of the ideas already listed)?
- If you couldn't use a car at all on that night, what might you do?
- What would happen if you did any of these things in reverse order?

These types of questions are based on an idea stimulating technique by Bob Eberle called SCAMPER. The technique helps students generate new ideas by asking them to consider how they might substitute, combine, add, magnify (minimize), put to another use, eliminate, or reverse an idea.

After the class has generated many ideas, invite them to call out the ones they think will be fun. Place a check by the ideas your students identify as fun. Then ask the students to call out the ideas which will be inexpensive. Again, place a check by the ideas that are called out.

Explain to the students that at this point you have used the questions, "Will it be fun?" and "Will it be inexpensive?" as *criteria* to evaluate their ideas. Ask the students what other criteria they might use to narrow the list. Explain that criteria often relate to costs, time, feasibility, acceptability, and usefulness. Then, write their suggestions for criteria on the board.

After the class has generated five or six criteria for evaluation, take a moment to check for understanding. Each student should understand what criteria are and that they are used to evaluate ideas.

Next, pass out a copy of the evaluation grid (page 125), and move students into groups of four or five. Ask the groups to pick four of the criteria from the board and write them above the lines labeled "Criterion" on the evaluation grid. Then, ask the students to pick the four most promising ideas for a Saturday night from the board's list. Have them list those ideas in the column labeled "Ideas." You may need to model the process either on the board or using an overhead.

Next, explain that using one criterion at a time, they should rank their ideas from 1 (best) to 4 (worst). Remind them to complete the ranking for one criterion at a time before moving to the next (i.e., move up and down the grid not across). Also, encourage the groups to modify ideas in order to increase their score.

Once they have completely filled out their grids, the groups should total the scores for each idea. Explain that the lowest score is the idea that ranks strongest for the selected criteria. The best score possible would be four and the worst possible would be sixteen. Again, if there is any confusion at this point, you may need to model the process.

When all groups are finished, have a speaker from each identify the criteria they used and describe the perfect Saturday night for the entire class.

Complete the lesson by reviewing the steps involved in productive thinking —

- Generate ideas using brainstorming
- Follow the five rules of brainstorming
- Generate and select criteria for evaluation
- Evaluate ideas using criteria on an evaluation grid

Close the lesson by explaining that the students will now use this new thinking process in a simulation where they play characters living in the future.

The Simulation

Preparation
- Arrange your room to accommodate small student groups of 4-5 students each
- Make copies of simulation handouts (pages 119-125) for each student
- Make one copy of the evaluation grid for each student

Introduction
Before you read the remainder of these instructions, skip to the participant's handouts (pages 119-125). These handouts give the necessary historical background and situation information.

1. Begin the simulation by reviewing the steps involved in the generation and evaluation of ideas. Make sure that the class understands the rules for brainstorming and the use of the evaluation grid.
2. Introduce the simulation by giving a copy of handouts 1 and 2 and the evaluation grid to every student. Then allow about 20 minutes for the students to read over the simulation's instructions, historical information, and couples' profiles.

3. Organize the class into small groups of 4 to 5 students. Explain to the groups that when they are finished, a speaker from the group will present their findings to the rest of the class and explain the criteria they used to make their decision.
4. Allow the student groups to begin work. Circulate among groups to answer questions.
5. When all of the groups have made their final decisions, ask a speaker from each to identify the couple they chose and the criteria they used to make their decision.
6. When all of the groups have presented their results, lead the class in an open forum discussion of the following questions —

- Given the problem the people in the simulation faced, do you feel the CGC was their best available solution?
- Can you think of some possible social problems the CGC might create?
- What are some advantages of having a group such as the CGC in charge of childbirth?
- If you were going to evaluate the effectiveness of the CGC, what are some criteria you might use to form your evaluation.
- Does a government have the right to limit the number of children you have?
- What are some alternative ways of managing this problem?
- Do you feel that using the evaluation grid improved the quality of your group's decision?
- What were some frustrations you experienced when using the productive thinking process?
- What are some of the strengths of using the productive thinking process?

Joel McIntosh is currently the editor of The Prufrock Journal *and working toward his doctorate at Baylor University (Waco, Texas).*

For The Common Good—Simulation Handouts

History

In the winter of 1994, a German scientist announced that he had discovered a process for ending human aging. When the process was performed upon a human zygote (the earliest developmental stage of a fetus), the resulting individual would live a life free from the effects of old age. While most of those treated would eventually die from disease or accident, their average life spans would still be over 400 years.

While the news sounded exciting at first, governments began to worry. At the time, the world's population stood at over 5.7 billion and was increasing by almost 90 million a year. In an already crowded world, the idea of unleashing a process that prevented death by aging was frightening. Such a process foretold a horrible future. Under such conditions, shortages of food, clean water, energy, and other resources would reach crisis proportions. Human life would be little more than a cramped, joyless existence.

Fearing such a future, world leaders acted. Acting through the United Nations, the leaders of the world established the Council for Genetic Control (CGC). The CGC was given control of the new genetic technique, and the sole authority to determine who should receive the treatment. As the process has to be performed on a human zygote, the only way for the CGC to make such a decision is to evaluate the parents of the potential offspring. The United Nations granted each of its member-nations a branch of the CGC with specific quotas based on population, available resources, and other relevant factors.

The American CGC is limited to choosing only 100 couples a year. In a complicated process repeated 100 times each year, CGC computers pick five promising couples from those who have applied. The information provided by these couples is then used by the American CGC to choose a single couple from the five who will be allowed to have an ageless child.

Because ageless humans may bare children throughout their long lives, a single individual might be responsible for fifty or more children. Clearly, in the distant future, a majority of the human race may be able to trace its lineage back to the couples picked by the CGC. The choices the CGC makes are very important.

Instructions

In this simulation, you and your classmates play the part of members of the American CGC. To make the best decision possible, you will meet in a small group and choose five criteria for evaluating the five couples' applications (list these on page 124). You will then use an evaluation grid (page 125) as a group to evaluate the couples and choose one whose child may receive the new process.

Couple 1

Wife's Name: Maria L. Benavides
Occupation: Free-lance Photographer
Age: 24
Intelligence: Above Average
Race: Hispanic
Education: BA in Journalism
Goal: Own and run a photography studio
Medical Background: Maria is an excellent athlete who was involved in many high school sports.
Personal Information: Maria is a highly creative person whose work in photography is highly valued. She is also actively involved in environmental issues and has recently become interested in local politics.
Husband's Name: Benjamin Benavides
Occupation: Computer Programmer
Age: 25
Intelligence: Above Average
Race: Hispanic
Education: BS in Computer Science
Goal: Own and run his own software company
Medical Background: Ben's father died of heart disease at 38, and his mother developed terminal cancer at age 56.
Personal Information: Ben is a highly motivated computer programmer. Because of his exceptional, almost genius, skills in math and computer programming, he is highly valued by his present employer.

Couple 2

Wife's Name: Veronica Ladd
Occupation: Newspaper Reporter
Age: 25

Intelligence: Above Average
Race: Black
Education: BA in Journalism
Goal: Become a reporter for a major daily newspaper
Medical Background: Veronica is a carrier of sickle–cell anemia. While she does not suffer from the disease, there is a *small* chance that her children will.
Personal Information: Veronica is a very good reporter with whom her superiors are impressed. She enjoys her job and is involved in a number of community activities.
Husband's Name: Mark Ladd
Occupation: Lawyer
Age: 33
Intelligence: Above Average – Genius
Race: Black
Education: Law degree
Goal: Become a U.S. senator
Medical Background: Mark is an exceptional athlete who played on tennis and soccer teams in both high school and college.
Personal Information: Mark is a well respected and well liked individual. He has argued a case before the Supreme Court. Many fully expect him to realize his goals and, perhaps, exceed them.

Couple 3

Wife's Name: Joanne Lau–Peck
Occupation: Founder and Owner of Quest Toys, Inc.
Age: 30
Intelligence: Above Average – Genius
Race: Asian
Education: MBA in Marketing and Administration
Goal: Make Quest Toys America's largest manufacturer of children's toys
Medical Background: None Relevant
Personal Information: Joanne has a very strong, assertive personality. She is generally liked and respected by those who work with and for her. No one doubts that Joanne will achieve her goals.
Husband's Name: Jim Peck
Occupation: Department Store Manager
Age: 27
Intelligence: Average – Above Average
Race: White
Education: BBA in Management

Goal: Become a vice–president of the department chain for which he works

Medical Background: Jim's grandfather and uncle both died of heart disease.

Personal Information: Jim is a "people person." He enjoys working with others, and they enjoy working with him.

Couple 4

Wife's Name: Jan Weaver

Occupation: District Manager for a National Fast Food Franchise

Age: 24

Intelligence: Average – Above Average

Race: White

Education: High School Graduate

Goal: Jan would one day like to begin a home based mail–order business. She believes that by doing this she could have children and stay at home without sacrificing a second income.

Medical Background: Jan's family has a history of cancer of the reproductive organs.

Personal Information: Jan sees herself as a leader. She is highly valued by the company she works for because she has a natural ability to settle arguments and disputes among employees to everyone's satisfaction.

Husband's Name: Jack Weaver

Occupation: Foreman at Large Industrial Plant

Age: 23

Intelligence: Average

Race: White

Education: High School Graduate and Taking Night Classes at a Local Community College

Goal: Move into a management position at his company

Medical Background: Jack is in perfect health. At his high school, he played football and baseball and has managed to retain his physical fitness.

Personal Information: Jack enjoys people. Many of those who work under him at the factory see him as a true leader who will one day rise to powerful positions of leadership. He spends some of his free time coaching little league football and baseball teams.

Couple 5

Wife's Name: Anna Reynolds
Occupation: Physics Professor
Age: 27
Intelligence: Above Average
Race: Hispanic
Education: Ph.D. in Physics
Goal: Become head of physics department at her university and move the department toward more innovative research and teaching
Medical Background: None Relevant
Personal Information: Anna has some very innovative ideas about the science of physics. The most important of which is that she would like to see physics on the college and high school level taught in a more interesting and valuable way to more people. She wants the American population to understand, as she does, how exciting science can be.
Husband's Name: Randy McCabe
Occupation: Biology Professor
Age: 28
Intelligence: Above Average
Race: White
Education: Ph.D. in Biology
Goal: Randy loves the life of a research scientist. If given the chance, he would like to spend the rest of his working life researching in the laboratory and raising children with his wife.
Medical Background: Randy's father, a heavy cigarette smoker, died of lung cancer at age 49. Randy also smokes but says he wants to quit.
Personal Information: Randy is absorbed by his work. Though he is a loving and supportive husband, his real joy in life revolves around the discoveries he makes in the laboratory. Randy is a solemn individual who does not care for the company of more than a handful of friends.

List your criteria for evaluation:

Remember, each of the criterion below should begin with the phrase "To what extent ..."

Criterion 1:

Criterion 2:

Criterion 3:

Criterion 4:

Criterion 5:

Evaluation Grid
For the Common Good

Couples	CR 1	CR 2	CR 3	CR 4	CR 5	TOTAL

Our Relationship With The Biosphere
An Exploration Of the Wilderness
With Gifted And At-Risk Students

By Dr. Ben Wilson & Cynthia Wilson

Providing enriching educational experiences for all students, especially gifted students and at-risk students, is a challenge to educators throughout the country. Professional practitioners dealing with such youth are constantly thinking of activities, projects, or events that will have effective holding power and produce fruitful learning experiences. Such activities should be thought provoking, motivational, attainable, and provide new knowledge or reinforce that previously learned.

For at-risk students, a number of new programs designed to keep them in school have focused on tangible rewards and incentives. Many are sequenced for immediate delivery since long-range planning or lengthy preparation is rarely considered of value to these students.

The profile of the at-risk student is complex. One consistent characteristic included in the profile is that such students seldom participate in school activities and are not a part of a group outside school. Educators often stress the importance of encouraging these students to become part of group activities—to become an active part of a network of supporters and role models.

These heterogeneous groups of students offer an interactive forum for helping students develop acceptable social behavior, exercise leadership potential, and learn how the get along with others. The development of these skills in the context of group activities can be enhanced by group involvement in goal oriented activities.

Likewise, leadership training, development of self-awareness, and social skills development are important focuses for meeting the needs of gifted and talented students. Given these similarities of needs, bringing at-risk students and gifted students together in an enrichment activity promised positive results.

To offer just such an activity to both gifted and at-risk students, a pilot program involving a number of gifted and talented students and a number of at-risk students was designed and implemented at Jack C. Hays High School, Hays Consolidated Independent School District in Texas. The program goals included:

• to allow students the opportunity to be part of a group and participate in an activity with a diverse set of peers

- to provide an exciting educational experience having lasting, positive impact on the students involved
- to provide an experience which would cause potential dropouts to stay in school

The remainder of this article offers an account of this pilot program's implementation by Cynthia Wilson, one of the teachers involved with the program.

The Adventure

When I was a child, my sister, brother, and I were frequent "guinea pigs" for various projects my parents pursued. My mother became a fine seamstress, an excellent cook, and an impressive barber, sometimes at the expense of her children. My father used us to practice administering standardized tests and to try out the latest child psychology theories.

Not surprisingly, I emerged from adolescence as a somewhat curious adventurer, eager to try any new experience as long as it was legal, moral, and relatively safe. So, when I was offered the chance to take a group of teenagers on a five-day camping trip in the most remote and isolated part of the Texas wilderness, I immediately accepted. My colleagues questioned my sanity, but this was not an opportunity I planned to pass up.

This trip, organized by Ramos Olivas, Rudy Lopez, and Ben Wilson, Jr. (yes, my father, and yes, I am still a guinea pig), was the pilot outing for a program designed for a combination of gifted students and at-risk students.

First, we selected students for the project. As a teacher of gifted students, I had no problem finding gifted student-volunteers for the camping trip in my history classes. I ended up drawing four names from a hat.

I did not have much contact with students identified as at-risk. So, I asked our school's counselor of at-risk students for help. We came up with a list of about ten students. I met with them and explained the camping trip, and several seemed interested. The counselor met with those students, and he and I narrowed the list down to four. Unfortunately, one of the students dropped out of the trip the evening before the event, and I ended-up with fewer students than expected because I had no alternate. I will not make that mistake again.

Once we selected the group, the students and I met to discuss the trip. At this meeting, we took care of administrative issues (e.g., release forms, health forms, lists of needed supplies, etc.). With all prepared, all we had to do was wait for March 22—easier said than done! The students and I could hardly wait.

When that day finally arrived, four boys, three girls, and I loaded all our gear, food, and bodies into a van and left the school at 6:00 a.m. We drove west for about ten hours and arrived at Big Bend National Park. After a brief orientation meeting, we made camp at Rio Grande Village. After a supper that we cooked ourselves, we attended the first of several naturalist presentations planned for the weekend. Our first, "The Geologic Connection," prepared us for our few days and nights in the park by presenting an overview of several areas we were scheduled to visit.

The next morning, Friday, after breakfast, we took a guided nature walk in the natural Basin. Led by a knowledgeable young ranger, we learned to recognize various forms of plant and animal life in the park. Then we were off on our own to explore Dug-Out Wells and Panther Pass, testing ourselves on what we had leaned so far. The climate of these areas of Big Bend resembled that of a desert.

After a picnic lunch at the a camp lodge, we explored a higher and cooler part of the park—the Lost Mine Trail. As part of our project, the students cleaned the trail of any litter they found. The students found little—the hikers before us had cared enough to "take only pictures and leave only footprints."

The entire day had been windy, and when we returned to camp, we found that the winds had broken the poles of one of our tents and had collapsed the other two. The students worked together with few tools to repair the campsite. The night before, some of the boys had spotted some bamboo stalks, and one of the at-risk girls suggested using the stalks as splints for the poles. With knives and duct tape the group worked together to solve the tent problem.

After a late-night presentation in the Big Bend Amphitheater designed to prepare us for the next day's trek, we bedded down for the night.

On Saturday morning, we headed for Boquillas Canyon for a nature walk entitled, "Resource Management at the Park." After the presentation we hiked the short distance to the Rio Grand river—the natural boarder between the United States and Mexico. There, we were delighted to discover a row of "river taxis" ready to take us across the river to Boquillas, Mexico.

While in Boquillas, our visit to a school sparked a good deal of interest among my group. Though the students found the primitive nature of the institution surprising, they were most surprised to find that the school offered only grades one through six.

While in Boquillas, the students sampled the culture. They traveled the streets, ate at a local outdoor cafe, and even watched the slaughter of a goat in preparation for a festival the next day.

After returning across the river, our group traveled to the Hot Springs area of the park. Later that night we attended the "Streamside to Summit" naturalist presentation given in anticipation of the next day's river rafting excursion.

The next day's river rafting excursion, however, turned out to be quite an adventure. During the rafting trip, the wind rose dramatically. Gusts were so strong on the water that we could paddle with all our strength and do little more than remain still in the water. Finally, we took turns tugging our boats, pretending to be Humphrey Bogart pulling his African Queen.

Wet, tired, and hungry, we pulled our rafts ashore before we had reached our camp site. By the time transportation came for us, we were too late for the final naturalist presentation, "Wings at Night." But our adventures had left us too tired to care, and none of us had trouble falling asleep.

The next day, we left Big Bend Park with plenty of stories to tell and each with a patch and certificate for completing the "Biosphere" program.

Yet, the students left with so much more. They left with a special concern for the environment. They left with an appreciation for the talents and abilities of each member of the group—with a greater sense of self worth for contributing to the challenges of our survival in the wilderness.

Of course, the trip's most valuable results came at the beginning of the next school year when all the at-risk students on the trip sought me out to let me know they were still in school. The seven students on the trip often mention some aspect of the trip each time I see them. The sparkle in their eyes lets me know that the experience we shared, the understanding and appreciation for nature and each other we gained, will be with us for a very long time.

Dr. Ben Wilson, Ms. Cynthia Wilson are educators of many years. They along with Rudy Lopez will present their "Biosphere" project in detail at the fall conference of the 1991 Texas Association for the Gifted and Talented in Dallas, TX.

Unlock Your Doors For All Kids
An Innovative Disability Awareness Unit
For Your Gifted Classroom

By Carolyn Rancier

While evaluating the year with my gifted and talented students, a theme surfaced. They wanted 'hands on experiences' doing service projects in the community and to research real problems.

Immediately, "Kids on the Block" came to mind. Kids on the Block is an organization which utilizes full-body puppets and Bunraku puppetry techniques. Bunraku puppetry originated in Japan. The puppeteer stands directly behind the puppet to manipulate it. Kids on the Block perform shows for 4th grade classrooms to promote disability awareness. Because I had been involved with the program, I knew our regional educational service center, which was now in charge of Kids on the Block, needed volunteers to perform with the program. Why couldn't my gifted and talented students take over this project?

Since the passing of the mainstreaming law (Public Law 94-142), educators have learned that integrating disabled kids takes more than just preparing the handicapped students. Our non-disabled students need to prepare as well. With this in mind, I approached the school administration and the educational service center with my plan.

The green light was given and I developed my Disability Awareness Unit. The unit provides students with the opportunity to do investigative exploring, utilize higher level critical thinking skills, and be of service to the school system and the community. The design of the unit is similar to that found in George Betts' *Autonomous Learner* where the teacher and students' relationship changes to that of co-learners.

As preparation, my students researched disabilities. Later, our performances began. After each performance, my students answered questions from the audience about the disabilities.

Kids on the Block usually is performed by adults. We were the first student performers in our state. I discovered that students operating the puppets added legitimacy to the act. It also provides students with an excellent opportunity for peer teaching and exposure to role models.

All involved with our disability study were greatly touched by the gifted and talented students' passion and dedication for enlightening other children and adults about disabled kids. One of my gifted students, Michael Stone, in an interview with the press said, "I used to play with a handicapped friend, but I felt uncomfortable. Now, I feel much better. These puppets have taught me a lot about character, self-esteem, and friendship."

With this article, I have included four strategies for teaching disability awareness. I would like to encourage teachers to incorporate some type of disability awareness in their curriculum. It is a wonderful opportunity to utilize administrators, parents, community leaders, and other students in your gifted program.

Disability Awareness Strategies

Strategy A: Kids On The Block

Objective: Students will develop communication, critical thinking, and Bunraku puppetry skills.

Procedure: After studying and learning Bunraku puppetry techniques, researching disabilities, and memorizing scripts, students perform puppet shows for 4th grade students. Each show will consist of two scripts between disabled and non-disabled puppets. Some educational service centers already have the Kids on the Block puppets and scripts which may be checked out. If yours does not, students can design and make their own puppets and write their own scripts.

Strategy B: First Impressions

Objective: Students will learn not to judge people by the way they look or by the way they act.

Procedure: Using Charles Allen Gilbert's picture, *All is Vanity*, a picture that at first glance appears to be a skull but which turns out to be a woman sitting at a vanity table, the students will brainstorm first impressions. A copy of *All is Vanity* may be purchased for a nominal fee from The Southwest Parks & Monuments Association, Lyndon B. Johnson National Historic Site, P.O. Box 329, Johnson City, Texas 78636.

Strategy C: Intimate Talks

Objective: Students will develop interpersonal communication skills.

Procedure: After investigating community resources for the handicapped, students will conduct interviews and arrange field trips or guest speakers for the class.

Strategy D: Wearable Art

Objective: Students will learn design and marketing skills.

Procedure: A cooperative venture will be formed by students and a local t-shirt company. The students design, make, and market t-shirts with a logo which promotes disability awareness.

Carolyn Rancier teaches a pull-out program at Franklin Middle School Abilene, Texas 79603. She plans to experiment with and expand this unit further.